MW01593526

BACK TO BASICS

HOW TO HELP YOUR CHILD BECOME A SUCCESS IN SCHOOL

by Paul Hollingsworth, Kenneth Johns, and Shane Templeton

MONARCH PRESS

NEW YORK

Published by Monarch Press
A Division of Simon & Schuster, Inc.
Simon & Schuster Building
Rockefeller Center
1230 Avenue of the Americas
New York, New York 10020
MONARCH PRESS and colophon are registered trademarks of
Simon & Schuster, Inc.
Designed by Irving Perkins Associates
Manufactured in the United States of America
1   2   3   4   5   6   7   8   9   10
Library of Congress Catalog Card Number: 85-61334
ISBN: 0-671-55557-X

CONTENTS

PREFACE

THIS IS A book for you, the concerned parent.

Although innumerable demands are made on you, both professionally and personally, you nevertheless want to be as supportive of your child's education as possible. This is not a book that will tell you how to teach your child. It is a book, however, that will help you to prepare your child for school and, once he or she is in elementary school, will help you support your child's development knowledgeably. Surprisingly, much can be done in your supportive role that does not require a great deal of time. This small investment on your part, however, will reap considerable rewards in terms of your child's understanding the traditional "basics": reading, writing, and arithmetic.

As you explore your supportive educational role with us, it will be important to bear in mind that learning is something that your child does all the time. Children cannot *keep* from learning—that is the way the human organism is set up. Your role as a parent will be to help facilitate that learning—to define what is most important and beneficial in the areas of reading, writing, and arithmetic. In so doing, you will be helping to develop attitudes towards learning that will remain with your child for the rest of his or her life.

You will find that, although we have written with different voices, we share a common psychological and philosophical premise. Our belief is: You can make a difference. You can make a significant qualitative contribution in your child's learning development.

To work with you toward this end, we have partitioned the book into three sections: "Readiness: The Preschool Years"; "A Good Start: The Primary Grades"; "Moving Ahead: The Upper Grades." We conclude with the Prologue rather than an epilogue because your child's growth up to this point is only the beginning. Success during the preschool and elementary years is the surest guarantee that your child will move forward to educational and career experiences that are intellectually and emotionally satisfying.

It is possible to approach the reading of this book from either a "sampling" or an "immersion" approach. You may choose to read only the material that is directly relevant to your child at this particular point in time, or you may wish to read the whole book, reflecting on where your child has been and getting a "feel" for where he or she has yet to go. Regardless of your approach, we believe that you will find much that is interesting and exciting—largely because of its simplicity and common sense. Indeed, there is very little that is truly new in education; quite often, however, we become overwhelmed with apparent "newness" and educational fads and lose sight of the simpler truths of teaching and learning. These truths, in the context of reading, writing, and arithmetic, we now wish to share with you.

PART ONE
Introduction

CHAPTER **1 You *Can* Make a Difference**

You have the right to demand for your children the best our schools and colleges can provide. Your vigilance and your refusal to be satisfied with less than the best are the imperative first step. But your right to a proper education for your children carries a double responsibility. As surely as you are your child's first and most influential teacher, your child's ideas about education and its significance begin with you. You must be a *living* example of what you expect your children to honor and to emulate. Moreover, you bear a responsibility to participate actively in your child's education.

—*A Nation at Risk*

IT IS IMPORTANT for you to realize that you as the parent can make a difference in the education of your child. It is *you* who can develop within your child the feelings and attitudes that will make for success in and out of school. A mother of one of the authors of this book stated over and over again that teaching was a noble profession. She made these comments not in a demanding or an inappropriate way. That was how she felt about education and teachers, although she was not a teacher herself, and she freely expressed it in front of her four children. It is not surprising that eventually all of her four children became educators even though three of them prepared for careers other than teaching.

FIRST AND MOST INFLUENTIAL TEACHER

It has been a recognized fact that the parent is the child's first and continuing teacher. Whether or not the parent will be considered the most influential teacher will depend a great deal upon what the parent will do. In reading this book, you have already made one step forward in striving for this goal because it shows that you are concerned and interested about the educational factors affecting your child.

You can help your child by creating and maintaining a favorable educational environment. Your positive attitude about education, and your willingness to give of your *time* in creating this environment, will have many positive effects upon your child. Quality time is the essential ingredient; so don't worry if you have many other responsibilities that take your time, just make those few minutes that you do have really count. This book is written to give you ideas on how you can make those few minutes really count. Create a positive environment by having materials available and be willing to answer your child's questions about all and anything that comes to his or her mind.

CHILD'S IDEAS ABOUT EDUCATION

A child develops his feelings and attitudes about education from you. It is vital to always talk and show by your actions that education is important in your family. This can be done even if you have not had all the formal educational programs you wish you had. The most "educated" people are those who never stop learning. Graduation from a formal school program is called commencement because education is not ending but beginning in the

12

"real" world. This "real" world is the world of experience, acquisition, and application of new knowledge on a day-to-day basis. We have to give the child the attitude that education and learning continue forever.

Your good feelings and attitudes about learning will affect your child's good feelings and attitudes about learning. This positive environment will not only affect your child's self-concept, but will indeed help your child in all of the learning activities that will be faced during a lifetime. So-called "bright" or "average" children don't always succeed. Those children, however, who have parents that encourage and motivate them to reach for higher learning goals do in fact succeed.

It cannot be emphasized too strongly that children mature and learn at different rates. Research has clearly shown that children go through developmental stages at various points in time. Your child may spurt ahead or lag behind. Only the most extreme and long-standing deviations from the norm need the attention of school ancillary personnel or a physician.

Remember that your child most likely faces twelve to sixteen years of education. Everything is not going to be learned to perfection in the first year of school. It is not absolutely essential that each paper be perfectly correct and show complete mastery. Remember, too, your child is learning the alphabet, to read, print his name, find the lunchroom, get on the right bus, find his way home from school, learn the name of twenty-eight other children, form a line, go to recess, and on and on.

THE LIVING EXAMPLE

You are the living example in your child's eyes. You, no doubt, have heard the saying, "I can't hear what you say because your actions speak so loudly in my ears." You aren't the formal school-teacher, but your actions need to communicate to your child what you expect him or her to honor and to emulate.

You need to be interested in learning. You need to be interested in discovering answers to questions or problems. You need to be aware of current events. You must show your child the need you have to read, write, and use mathematics in your life. In short, you need to be the living example to make the difference in your child's life of learning.

PARTICIPATE ACTIVELY IN YOUR CHILD'S EDUCATION

It is a proven fact that parents who actively participate in their child's education will make a difference in the learning for that child. This does not imply negative participation such as blaming the textbooks, the schools, the teachers, or the principals for poor educational practices. Rather, this implies that active participation promotes a positive relationship with teaching and learning. As a parent you have your responsibilities and the teachers have theirs; but the educational practices that you use in your home, in complementing what is done in the preschool, school, or elsewhere, constitute the important and overriding factors that will help your child be a success in school and in life.

Press of Time

You, too, have needs and demands on your time. You are quite possibly a working parent or even a single parent. You may come home from work tired, grumpy, and needing a few moments of time to heal your own wounds. You may be preoccupied with such chores as planning the menu, fixing the meals, preparing clothes for the next day, or mulling over plans for the weekend. Interspersed with your personal concerns are the gems which your child has saved to share with you—the fight at school, the triumph at Show-and-Tell, the lost lunch box, the friend whose tooth came out in the middle of reading. To hear and respond to these gems is an important part of parenting. We will share with you in this book ways that will capitalize on the normal interaction time you have with your child in the day-to-day care giving.

14

Monitoring Progress

Throughout the school years, your child needs the support of a loving and caring parent or parents. An important contribution you can make to your child is listening. You can be sympathetic. When the misspelled words appear on the daily lesson or when missed math problems happen, you may say, "Well, it looks as if you missed a few problems on this paper. Don't worry . . . you'll understand it better soon." This does not mean you should not continue to watch to see if progress is made. It does mean that you should not instantly communicate alarm and start to provide extra work at home. If as the school year reaches the halfway mark, your child is still making the same errors, it is time to confer with the teacher.

A conference with the teacher is often helpful in diagnosing the actual degree of problems, or indeed, if problems do exist. Teachers are less likely to be emotionally involved in the child's achievement and will not view an unsuccessful paper as a permanent blot on the family crest. They also see the larger picture and can compare your child's progress with that of the rest of the children and with the norm. If problems do exist and parental help is suggested, the teacher may be able to provide suitable activities. If more serious problems are indicated, the teacher may recommend professional tutoring. Don't plan to tutor your own child! Unless you have great patience and the ability to separate your feelings from the success or failure of your child, you should leave tutoring to an emotionally disinterested third party. This is not to say that you should not help your child learn. Is this a contradiction? No, it is a difference in emphasis. This book is designed to help you *assist* your child to learn the basics.

SUMMARY

You can make a difference in the education and learning of your child. You do this through your active involvement in the daily learnings of your child. You do it through listening and sharing

15

the rationale of your daily activities as they relate to education.

Inasmuch as you are your child's most influential teacher, your example, attitude, and approbation of your child's efforts are increasingly important as he or she matures and acquires new skills and knowledge. The child's ideas about education are formed by his or her experiences with you and other significant care-givers. This attitude should be internalized so that the child will view education as a journey rather than a destination.

It is with a view toward this total attitudinal set that this book explores opportunities to interact with your child in the areas of reading, arithmetic, and writing.

PART TWO

Readiness: The Preschool Years

CHAPTER 2 Reading

The home of the child stands out as a vital influence in reading readiness.

READINESS IS A term used to identify the preparedness necessary for a child to cope with any learning task. Reading readiness is the necessary development that children need to prepare them for the task of reading. Readiness in reading begins at birth and continues throughout the life of an individual. Reading readiness that is done in a normal, interesting way, rather than an overly structured formal way, becomes an exciting and fun experience for your child.

BUILDING INTEREST

One-year-old Julia with book in hand backs up to her Daddy's knee and says emphatically, "Book! Book!" Which means: Daddy, I want you to put me on your lap and read this book to me. Julia has already learned the excitement of books and has had some interest developed in her since she was a baby concerning the value of books.

Read to Your Child

If you want to interest your children in reading, you should read to them and pay attention to them when they seem to be curious about books. From birth on, you should read to your child many kinds of simple, interesting books. These books can be books that are designed for babies or they can be poetry books, nursery-rhyme books, or other simple reading books. The books that are colorful, large, and easily managed with your child on your lap are the ones to select. As you read to your child show your genuine excitement about the book being read. No matter what books you may choose, however, the main purpose is to read a wide variety of material to your child, thus building his or her interest in books.

Be a Good Model

Another way to build interest in books is for you to be a good reading model at home. If you show no interest in reading and use the time when you are not busy with other things, such as watching television, your child will feel that reading is not as important as television and television will become a priority for him or her as well.

Many times the author has been reading the newspaper and has had his child sneak up on him and try to hit the newspaper, not only making a rather loud noise but certainly causing the intense reader some consternation. Of course, the child wants his attention or maybe the child wishes to be reading some book with his father. If you are caught in a similar situation, remember that you are acting as a good reading model and don't feel guilty about continuing to read.

Children like to mimic their parents. "Look, Daddy, I can read just like you," said four-year-old David, as he was sitting in his father's chair holding the newspaper and turning the pages, acting as if he were reading the newspaper. In his acting the child plays out what he has seen the role model do.

You provide another most important "model" for your child. Every time you read to your child, you are modeling the reading process—you are modeling the sound and the cadence of language in books. You will discover—if you haven't already—that your young child will usually desire the same book or story to be read repeatedly. After a while, you may be driven to distraction by this. Keep in mind, however, that these repeated readings are serving a most important purpose: Your child will eventually know that story by heart! Even though he or she is not really *reading*, he or she "tells the story" to the book, turning the pages at exactly the right point. Over a period of time, your child will begin to match the words on the page to the words he or she is speaking, and gradually his or her understanding of words and learning to read a few words will grow out of this memorization.

Provide Reading Materials

Reading books, magazines, and other types of reading materials should be readily available to the child. Book-cases and reading materials should be located so the child will have easy access to them. It is always depressing to visit a home which has ample supplies of reading material, but which are located so high that the child cannot get to them. Don't mind the pile of books on the floor, either. Your child is using books and that is exactly what you want him or her to do—even to the point of the child taking all of the books from the shelf. In fact, a child of one of the authors spent every night for three weeks doing just that—taking books off the shelf and stacking them in piles on the floor!

There are many children's book clubs that you may join to get books that are appropriate for your child. In addition, the supermarket, variety, and drug stores carry a supply of books that are helpful. If you wish *not* to buy books, you can always go to the public library. Whatever method you choose be sure you have an ample supply of children's books readily available.

21

ORAL LANGUAGE

Building interest in reading is essential for reading readiness, but also equally important is the oral language development during these preschool years. Children acquire their oral language competencies implicitly (subconsciously), without formal instruction, from their role models in the home. They develop a concise accounting of aspects of the sound patterns and processes and the grammatical rule systems of their language. Children make these rule systems their own by using language in their preschool years.

Developmental Stages

Lest you worry about your child's development of oral language, listed here is the typical sequence of oral language development found in most children:

1. At approximately twelve to fourteen months, the first recognizable words are spoken.
2. From eighteen months to two years, children begin to understand spoken language and respond to simple directions. New words are being added to their vocabulary rapidly and these words are being put into sentences.
3. At approximately three years of age, the children are talking and using words with greater intelligence. Their sentences contain three or four words.
4. Four-year-old children enjoy talking and experimenting with words.
5. The average five-year-old child will have a wide vocabulary and will be able to form sentences of six or eight words quite easily.

These oral language developmental stages can vary greatly among children; do not worry if your child is ahead or behind the stages. If you find gross differences between your child and these guidelines, however, you should have your child checked by a specialist in child development. These guidelines for oral language are given to you only to assist you in monitoring your child's oral language development.

Oral Language Environment

Children's language patterns are best developed by surrounding them with a rich oral language environment. When you as a parent read stories or poetry to your child every day, you are enriching his or her oral language environment.

Talk with your child individually and in family groups. In this way you will serve as an oral language model for your child and help in developing his or her language patterns. Not only should you talk to your child, but more importantly, encourage your child to talk to you. As your child talks to you, he or she will be learning how to express his or her thoughts orally. This is an important part of developing oral language.

A good oral language environment is one in which the child not only has an opportunity to listen to you and other family members talking, but one in which your child can spend time listening to stories on tapes or records. In this manner your child can hear other oral language models that will help to enrich his oral language environment.

Understanding Oral Language

The use of oral language is related to the mental development of your child. The words that your child uses represent ideas and concepts within his or her realm of knowledge. Many times your child may use words of which he or she does not necessarily understand the meaning. Thank goodness he *doesn't* understand some of these words he or she may repeat! During the preschool years your child will use words which you do not approve of in your family in order to get your attention or the attention of other adults. The best way to handle this problem is to avoid giving him or her a reaction that will reinforce the use of these words. Children need help in understanding the word meanings for the

23

words of which you do approve. This is why you need to work with your child in understanding the words that you want your child to know rather than assuming that your child understands them simply because he is able to repeat them.

During the preschool years, children like to say nonsense words that rhyme or just say a list of sensible words that rhyme. Your child may start out with a sensible word like "hay." And then repeat a list of words that rhyme such as: may, tay, way, lay, gay, vay, etc. Two nonsense words show up in this list along with sensible words. This type of development is normal and children enjoy playing with words in this manner. This should not represent to you that your child knows the meaning of these words any more than he or she knows which ones are the nonsense words. This is the moment when you can help them distinguish the difference, and at the same time develop meaning for the words that are sensible, without ruining his or her fun.

The easiest way to develop meaning for your child in these words is to discuss the words. Use them in many different ways by putting them into sentences, describing what each word means. Ask your child what he or she thinks the word means. Again, let's remember that you are not being asked to formally teach your child. In a friendly, interesting way, however, you are capitalizing upon the teaching moment for your child to be given experiences with words. These teaching moments may be done while you are busy doing some other household activity—just so long as you can talk at the same time.

LISTENING

Equally important in developing reading readiness during the preschool years is the development of listening skills. In fact listening and oral language parallel one another in your child's development. The child needs to learn to pay attention or to be able to attend to what is being said. Many parents feel that their child can listen well because he or she spends so many hours in front of the television. This is not necessarily so!

24

Attending Skills

One method used to help develop attending skills is to give your child an "advance organizer." An advance organizer is a statement from the parent which creates a mind-set in the child to prepare him or her for listening. An advance organizer helps your child to understand the nature of the listening skills needed before the act is required. For instance, you will say to your child, "I want you to listen carefully because I want you to do these *three things*. Go to the kitchen, get me the scissors, and bring me the paper on the table." The advance organizer for your child was in the first sentence, " . . . I want you to do these *three things*." This advance organizer helps your child to attend to *three* things. The use of the advance organizer also makes it possible for you to avoid needless demands for your child's attention.

Another way that you can help your child to develop attending skills is to speak in an interesting and animated manner. Speak as though you can hardly wait to tell your child something exciting. Avoid needless repetitions. Check with him or her to determine how well he or she understood what you said and then praise your child for paying attention.

A third approach in developing attending skills for listening is to be a good listener yourself when your child is talking to you. Your example as an excellent listening model will help to develop good listening skills in your child.

Listening Activities

There are many activities that you can do in your home that can aid in the development of listening skills within your child. Listed below are just a few listening activities that you can try:

1. Have your child close his or her eyes and then make some kind of a sound using a familiar object, like crumpling some paper, hitting two pieces of silverware together, making a noise with some familiar toy. Ask your child to identify each sound.

25

2. Have your child listen to stories on tapes or records and ask him or her questions about the stories heard.
3. Have your child listen to music and tap out the rhythm while the music is playing.
4. Give your child oral directions and have your child try to follow them.
5. Have your child close his or her eyes and listen to the sounds in the room or from outside the house. Then ask your child to describe the sounds heard.
6. Ask your child to tell you about sounds that he or she has heard. The sounds reported to you could be scary sounds, happy sounds, sad sounds, etc.
7. Have your child listen to you as you tell a story or relate an incident. Ask him or her questions about the story or incident. These questions could be: How does this story make you feel? What happened in the beginning, middle, and ending of this story? What was the boy, girl, or main character doing in the story? Where did the story take place? Would you like to do what this person in the story did?
8. In regular conversation you should expect your child to listen to you intently as you listen to your child intently. Not only will you serve as a role model in listening, but you will also help him learn vital listening skills.

Only a few activities have been listed for listening, but you can develop many more that can be fun for your child and at the same time increase his or her listening abilities.

Listening is a major skill for learning. This is an essential skill for reading readiness. These skills will develop your child's listening comprehension skills and thus will help him or her when reading comprehension is required when he or she enters school.

EXPERIENTIAL BACKGROUND

Experience-building for the preschooler is another reading readiness activity which is necessary for your child. Along with building interest in books, developing oral language and listening skills, providing experiences is another very important need for your child.

Three-year-old Adam asked, "Do we have an airpopper?" "What is an airpopper?" his father replied. Adam said, "You know, so we can use it with a ball." "How do we use it with a ball?" asked his father. "To pump it up," was Adam's exasperated reply. "Oh, what you mean is an airpump," said his father. "Yes," said Adam, "an airpopper."

Children are always experiencing what is going on around them. Children need these experiences to develop their vocabulary and concepts so that they can recall them later when they are thinking, reading, talking, etc. This is what is meant when one reads about experiential background: experiences which are necessary in the preschool years so children will be ready to read the materials when confronted with them as they enter school in kindergarten or first grade.

A most valuable experience for your child involves her or his understanding the relationship between print and speech. You can facilitate this understanding by writing down what your child says about a drawing or a particular activity. For example, suppose your child draws a picture and you inquire about it. Your child responds, "This is a truck." At the bottom of the drawing, you can then write *This is a truck,* pronouncing each word as you write it. Writing down what your child says in his or her own words goes a long way towards facilitating the print-speech relationship—and is quite exciting for your child!

Auditory and Visual Discrimination

Your child needs to recognize sounds to develop his or her reading readiness. Some of the activities that were mentioned earlier in this chapter can help, but in addition to these you may wish to discuss sounds of letters and words with your child. For instance, when the child is repeating words that rhyme you may use that opportunity to discuss why the words rhyme. What makes them sound alike? You may play a game with your child by giving pairs of words and ask him or her if the words sound alike, for example, bat - bed, bat - mat, etc. The first pair does not sound alike, but the second pair does. This type of gamelike activity will keep the interest of your child for some time.

BACK TO BASICS

Your child needs to be able to visualize and recognize different shapes, colors, sizes, and textures. Your child should be able to interpret pictures by telling you what he or she thinks is going on in the picture. Before your child enters school in kindergarten, he or she should be able to distinguish individual letters and recognize some words. At the market while shopping, you can have your child identify certain letters or words from cereal boxes or other familiar commodities that you use frequently in your home. He or she may learn the word "stop" from the stop sign, etc. You will need to plan activities that will provide these experiences for your child. Coloring books and shape and texture activities from materials you have in your house will do. These can be done in a game-like activity and your child will truly enjoy the activities.

Directionality

Eye-hand coordination activities are also necessary for developing experiential background necessary in the reading readiness process. Play activities such as cutting paper, finger painting, working with clay, stacking blocks, painting with crayons, watercolors, and other types of media will help your child develop eye-hand coordination. There are many activities readily available in the home that can help in developing this skill, such as stacking plastic glasses or spoons.

Not only should you be concerned with eye-hand coordination, but also with developing the child's method of looking at and observing objects, pictures, models, etc. While a child is developing in the preschool years it is not apparent how he or she identifies an object. Take an object such as a book. If your child looks at it upside down, left to right, right to left, top to bottom, or bottom to top, that object is always the same—a book. It is only in the reading process that directionality is so important. Take for instance the letter "b." It is a "b" when one looks at it from left to right. It becomes a "d" if it is observed right to left, or it could become a "p" or "q" depending in which direction your child attacks the letter. In the reading process one must read from left to right; therefore, during these preschool years, it will be of great benefit to your child to develop his or her abilities in observing or looking at pictures or objects in a left to right direction. You can develop your child's attention in a left to right direction by simply drawing your hand across the picture in a left to right direction as you talk about the picture, object, or model. This can be done in a matter-of-fact way. In this way your child will learn to observe left-to-right direction subtly.

Concept Development

In concept development, your child should be able to understand concepts such as up and down, top and bottom, low and high, front and back, first and last, slow and fast, beginning, middle, and end, near and far, etc. These experiences for your child can again be game-like in nature. Try to use every opportunity to reinforce these concepts with your child. You can say, "This is the front of the book. This is the back of the book." It is very simple to work on concept development with your child when you are doing any activity at home, in the grocery store, or in the car.

Your child needs to have experiences that only you can give, such as trips to the supermarket, zoo, park, swimming pool, carnival, etc. These experiences are important, not only for his or her enjoyment, but for the background of knowledge that he or she needs for reading. It is important that not only is your child experiencing these trips, but that he or she is discussing with you about what he or she is experiencing. Even television can help as long as your child does not become a passive viewer. You should continually discuss with your child what is being viewed. Active participation is necessary on the part of your child to be able to get the type of experiential background needed for reading readiness.

SUMMARY

A parent called a university reading clinic and asked, "What should I do with my child? He has a 160 I.Q." The reading clinic director asked, "How old is your child?" The parent replied, "He

29

is three years old." The reading clinic director then said, "Play with your child and develop his reading readiness by doing. . . ." Before the last of the statements could be made, the indignant parent hung up the telephone with a loud bang. What the parent was trying to convey to the director was that his child was so bright that the reading clinic should start to formally teach his child to read right now. What the reading clinic director was trying to convey to the parent was that this was the time to work on building interest in reading, developing the child's oral language and listening skills, and giving the child a great amount of different types of experiences so when the child does enter school the teacher will be able to formally begin instruction for reading.

The important thing to remember from this chapter is to have a great amount of reading readiness activities for your child and to do it in a way that will be fun. No one wants to have a child bored about reading before he or she begins kindergarten or first grade. Remember, too, that the home is the most vital influence for reading readiness. You as the parent can make major differences in readiness by planning ahead what types of experiences and books you will have available and *how* you will spend your quality time with your child.

CHAPTER **3 Writing**

> Young children surrounded with spoken lan-
> guage will learn to talk ... and young children
> surrounded with written language will learn to
> write.

"PRESCHOOL CHILDREN *writing*? That's impossible!"

As anyone knows who has looked at the preschool child's scribbles or tried to deal with the request of a three- or four-year-old to "read what I writed," these young children's "writing" is a far cry indeed from what we usually think of when we think of writing. But unless we consider what children do in school as "writing" and what they do before they go to school as "not writing," then we should be able to see that the movement from scribbles to script is all part of the same process and that, yes, preschool children do indeed write.

For many years, the belief that preschool scribbles were not "real writing" blinded most of us from seeing the rich store of information that children expressed in their written attempts. At the age of two, for example, your child probably produces writing that looks like this:

BACK TO BASICS

By the time he or she begins kindergarten, it may look like this:

RCRBKDTD

(Our car broke down today)

Quite a change, and all without the benefit of "formal" instruction.

YOUR ROLE AS A MODEL

As was pointed out in Chapter One, your child will learn much about print from the environment—he or she is surrounded by it. For most children, however, simply being surrounded by print is not enough. They need to have their attention drawn to it. Your child, in other words, will benefit from your pointing out print, commenting about it, and, occasionally, discussing it. So, too, with writing.

We write a lot more than we usually realize. Think for a moment about approximately how many times a day you engage in the act of writing. You're probably not working on the next great novel, of course, but you *are* writing. Consider these situations: making out a shopping list, jotting down a bit of information while on the phone, doing a crossword puzzle, writing a note to the milkman, addressing cards to friends and family during the holiday season, measuring a window frame and writing down the dimensions, writing checks to pay the bills (perhaps figuring a column of numbers in the process). When we think about it, we realize we actually *are* writing quite a bit during each day. Your child is, as usual, curious about these written situations and will ask questions and probably "act out" these situations in play. You are, in a very real sense, a *model* for your child.

Older brothers and sisters are also models. In one of the author's families, the youngest child began at the age of eighteen months to imitate her two older brothers as they lay on the living room floor and wrote; she was observed to stare intently at her brothers, then lie just as they did (on her stomach, propped up on two elbows). She then would place her tongue between her teeth and slightly to one side, just as they did. *Everything* about the act of writing, in other words, was imitated—at her age, the most important thing obviously being how she situated herself. This is not unlike the young child who imitates the adult driving the car by furiously turning the steering wheel left and right—not realizing that this is but one of many things that the adult must do in order to control the car.

YOUR CHILD "INVENTS" A WRITTEN LANGUAGE

Because you probably read and write with such apparent ease, it may be difficult to realize what an amazing feat it is for your child to conceptualize how written language "works." How does your child come to the understanding that those marks on the page *stand for* something else, something that bears no relationship to the marks themselves? Think about it for a moment: A picture of a pig looks like a pig, but the *word* "pig" does not look at all like the genuine item. How does your child learn that, although they bear no resemblance to a pig, the letters p-i-g *mean* the same thing as the picture of the pig? The process of learning this, although a fairly long one, nevertheless takes place rather naturally, with some support and guidance from you. Another way of considering this is to realize that, by the age of six or seven, your child will have developed an understanding of written language that, historically, took the human race thousands of years to develop.

Your child's understanding that the letters p-i-g mean the same thing as the picture of a pig is not the end point of development, however. There is yet another critical understanding that unfolds:

33

the *way* in which print represents speech. For a few thousand years in most writing systems, marks stood for syllables. The idea that each mark or letter could stand for an individual *sound* is, historically, a late development—and it is no accident that this idea occurs later, after much exposure to print, in your child. Let's look at the development of this process and, along the way, consider what you can do to help it along.

What the Scribbles Mean

At one point or another you've probably had to deal with the consequences of crayons, magic markers, finger paints, and pens. And what's worse, the consequences of this budding creativity most often seem to turn up on every surface except paper. Rather than threatening the child with putting up the writing implements for several days if he doesn't mend his ways (the authors know one parent who put the wooden blocks in the attic for three years because her three-year-old child didn't pick them up one day!), simply be sure that there is lots of paper around and that the child knows where it is. Any type of paper will do, including used computer paper, which is becoming much easier to obtain. The message should be clear that *paper,* not walls or bedspreads, is what we write on.

Your child's scribbling begins the unfolding of a process you will be observing: The development of writing in children flows from the "whole" to the "parts." That is, children begin with very general features of written language, such as wavy lines, and move eventually to letter-like forms and, finally, to words with spaces in between them and composed of letters that you recognize.

Your child is impressed first with the general structure or appearance of print and, from this, gradually comes to produce the much more specific writing that we all would *recognize* as writing. Your three-year-old child may surprise you; if he or she has had occasion to observe you making out a shopping list, try requesting some time that he or she write a shopping list while you are making out one. You could very well get something like the following:

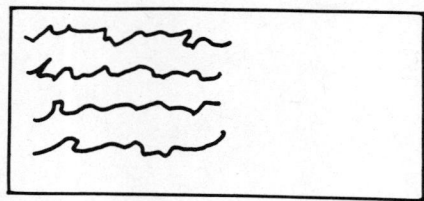

You may wish to compare this shopping list to a "story" that your child may spontaneously write at this age or which you may be able to coax him or her to write:

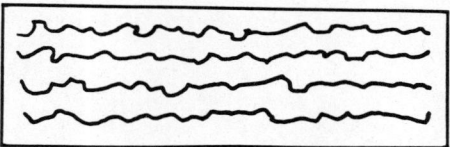

Surprised? You have probably not taught your child these differences, but he or she nevertheless has noticed them, thanks to your "modeling": the writing on shopping lists usually does not go all the way across the page; in storybooks and most other writing, however, it does. If you are a careful observer, you may be surprised by something else: Your child *may* begin at the left of the page and make the line from the left to the right, then return to the left-hand side again! This "directionality" may not always be so consistent—as we'll see below, children often reverse their writing and the direction in which they write—but this is an impressive example of what your child is capable of picking up from your modeling.

One day you may notice that the aimless squiggles your child has been churning out look vaguely familiar. What do you notice about the following "writing" of a four-year-old child?

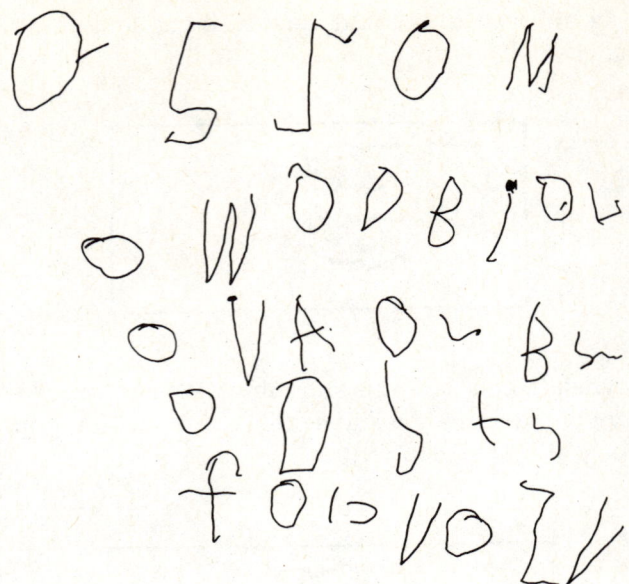

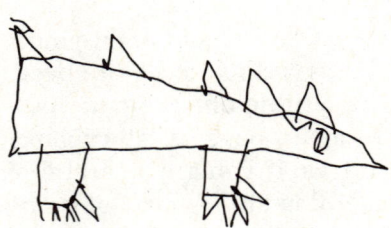

Do you see the letter-like shapes? How about that upside-down-and-backwards "Q"-type shape? This emergence of letter-like shapes is bound to happen; this child has been exposed to print and is doing what comes naturally—beginning to include features of this writing in his own efforts.

Although there are many things that preschoolers seem to do in common with regard to their writing attempts, there are also some "individualistic" things they will do. For example, several children seem to match their "writing" to reflect more directly the features of the real world that they are attempting to say something about. The following is a sample from a four-year-old child:

This child explained that the large glob said "dog" and the small glob said "puppy." He seems to be telling us, in his writing and in his explanation, that he understands writing "stands for" things out there in the real world but that writing does not really need to look exactly like what it is representing. He can't quite seem to give up this last idea entirely, however, so he keeps the feature of "size" in his writing. Notice that "dog" is written larger than "puppy." Here's another example of a similar strategy you may encounter:

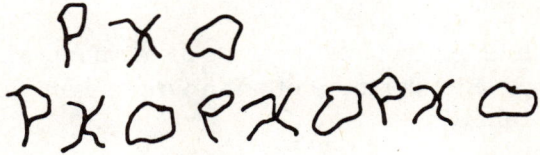

The child who wrote this explained that the first line said "duck" and the second line said "ducks." Not a bad try, and certainly quite logical! In effect, if you've got more "things" to refer to—in this case, ducks—then you need more letters; furthermore, for this child there is a definite order to the words.

The Role of the Child's Written Name

Your child's name is one of the most powerful and important guides he or she has in the process of "inventing" the way spoken language is represented in print. That single written word is imbued with all of the power of your child's awareness of self and is, perhaps more so than any other printed message, of truly magical proportions. In print, children are as "big" as anyone or anything else. Their written name can be traced, copied, and studied a thousand times. They begin to match the names of letters they are learning to the letters in their name—not always a perfect match, of course, but they are getting valuable information nevertheless. The budding understanding of how letters stand for sounds in words may begin here, and children may in turn begin to try to "spell" other words using letters and their names. In Chapter 1 the "lap method" of reading was discussed—so effective, yet so natural. It is in this context, too, where your child's written name can be introduced. Sitting at a table with your child in your lap, simply say, "Let's write your name." Pronounce their name, then write it, saying each syllable as you do. (Later you may vary this with saying the name of each letter as you write it.) Pronounce their name again, drawing your finger along underneath it from left to right. Later on, you can point to the beginning of their name and *tell* them, "This is the *beginning* of your name"; in the same manner you can tell them about the *ending* of their name.

As your child experiments with his or her name and begins to use recognizable letters more often in writing, you may one day observe the following:

YЯAM

What's happened? Your child, who previously was writing her name correctly from left to right, has reversed the process completely, including writing letters backwards! Do not be alarmed, however; this is quite normal and occurs in a great many children. As your child continues to write and you continue to model the direction of print as you read, the left-to-right directionality and order will reappear. Reversed letters, as a matter of fact, are a common occurrence in first graders; contrary to what some people believe, this does not usually mean that a child has a "learning disability" or is "dyslexic." One should only be concerned if this behavior, along with some other obvious signs of disability, persists for a long period of time.

The Role of the Alphabet

Is this the point at which children should learn the alphabet and, if so, how? Or, should they be left to pick up the names of the letters on their own? Does learning the alphabet song and the names of letters help children very much? Simply learning to parrot the names of the letters with no opportunity to use that knowledge probably does not help much; if children are allowed to *apply* that knowledge in their writing, however, then it is a rich source of information indeed. Programs like *Sesame Street* and *Mr. Rogers* do a fine job of teaching letter names; they may be one of the primary reasons why more children in recent years enter kindergarten and first grade already knowing their alphabet. It is not necessary, however, for young children to know all of the names of the letters for them to use this knowledge in their writing. Armed with just a few letter names—most significantly, those that occur in their own names—they will apply this knowledge in their writing. At first, as was pointed out above, there is no real relationship between the letters the children put down on the page and the sounds the letters represent—the children are simply writing them for their own sake. Gradually, however, they will become more logical in their use of the letters. Knowing her name (Carrie) and a few other letters, for example, a five-year-old child wrote the word "berry" as BRRIE.

As children sort through the information about print, their use of the terms involved with print will strike adults as quite amusing. They will use the terms "letter" and "word" interchangeably, and in fact will say that all sorts of things are words—"things that our mothers tell us," "when I do something," "things that come out of our mouths." All of this overlapping information becomes sorted out, however, as they are read to and as they continue to write.

When "Writing" Looks More Like Writing

Let's examine what happens in preschool children's writing after they are including letters fairly regularly in their efforts. The following message accompanied Gavin's (age five) drawing of a wintry scene:

$$LLK4TR$$

The "translation" of this is "I like winter." Although Gavin obviously has lots to learn about English spelling and the fact that we put spaces between words, consider how rich his efforts are. Using the names of letters, he has "sounded out" what he wants to say. "I" is of course spelled correctly. "Like" is spelled LK—not bad! "Winter" is spelled YTR; Gavin's use of the letter Y to spell the sound we hear at the beginning of *winter* is actually a pretty good choice. When we say the name of the letter *y* we hear the same sound as that which occurs at the beginning of *winter*. Gavin has no real reason to use the letter *w* because the *name* of that letter ("double-you") is nowhere near the sound he hears at the beginning of *winter*. What Gavin has done, then, is to select a letter whose name is closest to the sound he wants to spell—a very good strategy indeed for a child just beginning to learn about how we represent sounds with letters in the English language. Notice something else about Gavin's writing: with the exception of one obvious example ("I") he leaves out letters that stand for vowel sounds (the *i* in *like* and the *e* in *winter*). This is a very common phenomenon at this stage in children's writing. You needn't worry about your child "not hearing sounds"—if he or she has learned to talk, then they indeed can "hear sounds"! Rather, their task is to figure out *which* sounds need to be matched up with letters, and this will take some time.

You should also not be surprised if your child spends a great deal of time struggling to select letters to match the sounds he or she is uttering, only to be unable to read back what is finally written. The excitement here is so often in the *doing* of it. If you spend some time studying the ways that little ones spell, however, you may be able to read back to them what they have written—much to their intense delight. One of the authors spent a good deal of time one morning trying to figure out what "BBCUS" was (one of Gavin's efforts) and then when he hit upon it, it seemed so obvious: "Bye bye, see you soon!"

Now let's look at the note on page 42 written by Jason, another five-year-old child. Although you can probably "decode" the first line, you might be having some trouble with the rest. Would it help to know that the figure that seems to be wielding a battleaxe is not a fearsome warrior but is instead the tooth fairy and she is holding not a weapon but a magic wand? Jason was requesting precisely how much money he hoped to receive in exchange for his lost tooth: "May I please have a dollar?" In this piece of writing, we see that more vowels are included—some are sounded out and some, we suspect (such as the *a* in *HAV* and in *DALR*) are recalled from seeing the spellings in print. The *y* is used to stand for an "e" sound at the end of some words; for example, "Mary," "pretty." As this reasoning suggests, if you look closely you will see some fascinating details of your child's attempts to bring his or her own expectations about how words can be sounded out into line with the ways in which they see English acually spelled.

There is another aspect to this piece of writing that should be pointed out. Up to a point, so much of children's early writing is writing either for the sake or writing—the *act* is what is fun rather than the *function*—or for the purpose of simply labeling drawings. In the tooth fairy note, however, we see writing definitely being put to a *purpose*. It is sad to note that, for many children who do not write until they get into school, the idea that writing actually has a *purpose* never occurs to them—it is mere copying and most often an exercise in penmanship. On the other hand, children such as Jason who come to writing in a more natural fashion pick up this understanding with hardly any conscious effort at all.

At this point, children often use writing for a number of purposes—labeling, notes, directions, as well as stories. Their efforts may increase in length as well. The following composition was

written by a kindergartener in December, 1979, one month after over forty Americans were taken hostage in Teheran, Iran:

(I want the government to release the hostages. It is important the Ayatollah release the hostages. It is my command the Iranians to tell Ayatollah Khomeini to release the hostages.)

In addition to the obvious concern of this youngster for the welfare of the people being held hostage, there are some features of his writing that are of interest.

Notice the curious " " marks between some words. Whether these are parentheses, quotes, or what-have-you, we are led to ask what do they mean, what is their purpose? This child has probably noticed punctuation marks in print and, not knowing their purpose, assumes they obviously have something to do with writing. So, he includes them not where *we* might expect them to occur, but between words. Why? Actually, many children have been observed to put some sort of mark between words; it may indicate that they are beginning to notice that words have spaces between them (*not* an obvious feature to the nonliterate child) and that they are not run together. Prior to this point, children's writing does not usually include spaces—there are no "spaces" between words in speech, so why should the children include them in writing? But it is interesting that, even though the children are beginning to notice spaces in print, they often cannot bring themselves to put them in their own writing—it is almost as if they subconsciously don't want to "waste" any space on the page! Whereas this child used some type of punctuation mark, others have for example used dots, dashes, and diagonal lines.

Where did the phrase "It is my command" come from? Children usually do not use such language; what this child has done is quite common in writing—not long before, his parents had read a book to him in which a little prince repeatedly said, "It is my command" in order to have others do things for him. This child simply borrowed the phrase for his own writing. A more common example of this is children's use of the phrase "Once upon a time" to begin their stories—only in books is this language usually encountered.

Note the different ways the same word is spelled in this little story. "Release," for example, is spelled three different ways. Such variable spelling is quite common, and does not seem to faze young writers—unless adults make a big deal about it! It is perhaps best at this point, by the way, to address a concern often expressed by parents whose children are attempting to spell words this way by sounding them out: "Won't this lead to bad spelling habits later?" The answer is a resounding "No!" In fact, children who begin writing this way usually turn out to be *better* spellers. Why? They have more experience in analyzing spoken language for purposes of writing; quite simply, this experience provides a much richer soil in which correct spelling and understanding of the many features or words can later be sown.

Now that we have some idea of the marvelous strategies that preschool children are using to write, is it any wonder that one five-year-old child posted the following sign above his little work table:

Do NAT DISTRB GYNS AT WRK

(Do not disturb; genius at work)

A FINAL WORD

Several things have been suggested throughout this chapter that you can do to facilitate your child's development as a "budding author." Briefly, let's review them:

1. "Model" reading and writing for your child.
2. Be sure to have plenty of paper and writing implements on hand and that they are easily accessible.
3. Label things around the house; be sure that the print is at a height which your child can see easily.
4. Invite your child to write with you when you have occasion to write.
5. For the five- and six-year-old child, suggest topics and/or times that would result in some rewarding, fun writing.

6. Do *not* insist on "correct" spelling; this will in the long run dampen your child's interest in and exploration with writing.
7. Keep it fun! Your child may elect to go for some time— days or in some cases weeks—without writing; this, too, is quite normal. Don't unnecessarily goad or press your child to write. Although children may not be consciously picking up on adults' anxieties, intuitively they are and will become anxious themselves.

A note about microcomputers and preschool writing. Recall what was said about microcomputers and preschool reading in Chapter 1? The same goes for *writing* in the preschool child. Although experience with microcomputers is excellent for the preschool child, as yet there is no software that can come anywhere near doing what you can do so well: modeling aspects of how printed language works through reading to your child and through having him or her see you in the act of writing.

Young children *have* been observed composing in a word processing program; this is good experience, but unless you already have a word processing program do not run out and buy one solely for this purpose. It should be pointed out that *finding* the letter on the keyboard that stands for the particular sound a child wants to spell is not the same process as thinking of the letter on one's own.

Fortunately, many preschool and kindergarten teachers are aware of the intense research in recent years into young children's writing, and are providing for the sorts of experiences with print that have been described here. Children do *not* learn to write best by being taught how to make the letters—as we have seen, they actually work the other way 'round—from the general features of writing to the specific. Moreover, they do this with a *purpose*—either the joy of the act of producing marks or the intent to *do* something with what was written, to give it a *purpose*.

CHAPTER 4 Arithmetic

The mighty oak from a small acorn grows. So too, from small beginnings in arithmetic does great learning derive.

EARLY YEARS

THESE ARE THE pre-school years. These are the years when you may have the greatest opportunity to work with your child; greater than you may ever have again. These are the years where you will have the greatest influence on your child compared with that held by teachers or playmates in later years.

If you are a single parent do not feel that your child will be unable to compete because you do not have as much time as do other parents who do not hold full-time jobs. There is some evidence that early growth, early training of children's intellectual skills may result in no greater abilities in later life. That is, other children will catch up. Yet, there is also some evidence to suggest that this early training may set the stage, set a predisposition to learning that may not be measurable in the standard ways. You need to know that we authors are educators who feel no urgency to institutionalize the training of young children. Rather, we feel that parents with a minimum of available time can work with their children in a loving and fun-sharing relationship and accomplish many wonderful things in preparing the child to enter his or her workaday world called school.

There is much written these days about the parental rush to teach children beginning as early as three months. In one of these approaches a parent holds up a card for a second or two and says to the infant the word or the number of dots appearing on the card. This approach makes the assumption that the child will begin to associate the number of dots with the spoken numeral. However, researchers have found that infants do not distinguish between four and five objects at twelve to fifteen months of age and are not sensitive to addition, or subtraction, more complicated than 3 + 1 at twenty-five to thirty months of age. Since the author of this approach admits that there is no long-term research on this program, we neither advocate nor deny the benefits. We do recommend a program of lots of parent-child interaction reflecting a less formal, less rigorous approach. If you are interested in pursuing the teaching of arithmetic to your two-year-old, you should consult the book, *Teach Your Baby Math,* by Glen Doman, published by Simon and Schuster, 1979. In his book, Doman recommends you begin teaching your child at one or two years of age. Doman feels that any later time is getting beyond the optimum age.

According to pediatrician T. Berry Brazelton of Harvard, "Everyone wants to raise the smartest kid in America rather than the best adjusted, happiest kid."[1] There is some evidence to show that some of these intense, early training programs may be causing a great deal of stress and emotional harm to young scholars. This chapter will proceed from the standpoint that there is little that will substitute for a parent who is sensitive and caring, one who is willing to respond to the infant's need to be stimulated physically and intellectually.

The first section of this chapter will deal with this early development of your child. However, since whole books have been written on the subject, we can only offer a few of the most basic and beginning activities.

For the infant under six months of age one activity designed to develop the child's response mechanism is to touch the inside of

---

[1](*Newsweek,* Mar 28, 1983, p. 62)

the baby's hand. When your baby grasps your hand, let go. When baby drops it, produce your hand again. Enclose the baby's hand in yours, smile.

Another activity for developing the baby's sense of cause and effect relationships is to tie a scarf around your neck. Let it dangle over your baby. Shake the scarf so it will be noticed. Touch it to your baby's hand. When the baby touches the scarf or reaches for it, smile and talk to the baby. Do not talk too much. Talk in response to the baby's reaction.

Stimulate your baby's sense of touch and color by tying several different-feeling objects on a ribbon. Let the objects dangle near the baby. Bring one of them to the baby's hand so it can be grasped. Change the objects from time to time as the baby loses interest.

These are the kinds of activities that caring mothers and fathers, and caregivers in general, have been doing for as long as parenting has been going on. The point is that there is little substitution for interaction with the baby. Talk to your baby, say colors, shapes, textures, temperatures. Frequently bring new and different touching objects to the baby. Play games like peek-a-boo and "You talk, then I'll talk," games. Have a good time with your infant! Keep in mind your goal is to provide a variety of stimulating experiences. Respond emotionally when the baby shows a response to something you do. Robert McCall, in his book, *Infants,* stated that there are certain requirements for early learning. He says that infants first learn what is related to what they already know. For example, they learn best by looking, touching, and sucking. These are three activities they have done from birth. Secondly, in order for infants to change their behavior, something must happen to cause that change. That is, there must be some reward. A third requirement is that such encouragement or "reward" must be immediate. An example of reinforcing the infant's behavior is the exclamations of glee and joy by the parent when the baby first smiles, or grabs the hair. The immediate reinforcement produces further smiling or hair grabbing.

Fourth, the encouragement must be clearly associated with the behavior to be learned. That is, you must smile and talk to your baby immediately upon his or her initial gurgles, smile, hair grabbing, or whatever.

BACK TO BASICS

Finally, McCall reminds us that, like their parents, infants are individuals. Whether the infant is having a good time playing depends upon how well the activity is matched to the infant's behavior.

These activities may seem to be so simple one cannot help but wonder why more infants do not learn more rapidly. The problem may be that parents respond too slowly to the infant's action or they may respond on a hit and miss basis; one day the infant's behavior is lauded, the next day it is ignored.

GEOMETRICAL SHAPES

When your child is between the ages of one and one-half and three years old you should be teaching geometrical shapes. This is best done with the coordination boards found in infant's department or toy stores. This is the kind of board that has the brightly colored shapes cut out, and into which the child can place a triangle, a square, a circle, a rectangle, and so forth. Teach your child by identifying the qualities of triangle-ness, not by color alone. Say, as your child picks up the triangle, "That's a triangle, see, it has three sides. Let's count them, one, two, three. Notice it has a big bottom and a point at the top. Watch, if I turn it (here you rotate it one turn) it still has a big bottom and a point at the top." With each of the blocks describe the quality that makes it round, square, or rectangular. Do not, we repeat, do not make this a schoolroom lesson. This is a loving, play-oriented activity. The learning is to come second to the parent-child interaction. If your child shows signs of frustration or boredom, leave the activity immediately. It is better for your purposes to have your child wishing there was more rather than wishing it were over.

COUNTING

If you decide you wish to follow the Glen Doman procedures mentioned earlier, you are possibly well on your way to having your infant counting. If not, you should be aware of the following activities that a one-and-one-half- to three-year-old child can do: counting can be name calling; counting can be one-to-one correspondence; counting can be inclusive of all the objects counted.

Let us explain: We often hear children count to ten, but they do not attach the numeral to the object they touch. It is like saying a poem. This procedure is name calling. The child has learned the numerals by rote but with no meaning. Next, there is the child who, as he or she speaks a numeral, touches the corresponding object. Finally, there is the counting in which the last object touched and named covers all the preceding objects. In other words the child is aware that the numeral seven stands for seven distinct objects.

The first kind of counting, name calling, is one you can accomplish during this time. Again, make it a game. Start with games like counting the toes in musical tones. Start with "buzzing" your child. Point a finger, make the buzzing sound, circle the finger over the child, and tickle gently. After a couple of these episodes the child will anticipate the tickle and giggle with glee. The next time replace the initial buzzing with saying the numerals, 1, 2, 3 . . . then buzz. You've probably done this routine a dozen times already. The only difference is that this time you're preceding the buzzing with a set of numerals. As you continue to use numerals for items, have the child join in. Count out the child's blocks, potatoes, etc. Work on one through five, then five to ten. Always reinforce the original numerals by starting at one. Do not expect at this early age to have your child be accurate in one-to-one correspondence. That is, be satisfied with name calling. Rejoice if the child can tie the verbal "one" to the first object, "two" to the second object, and so forth. If he or she can bring you three potatoes at your request, you are even farther along.

BIG-LITTLE

The terms of relational value are the words big and little, and in arithmetic, more and less. To teach the big-little concept use three objects from the child's world such as three stuffed toys of obviously different sizes. Put the toys in a row, big on the left, small on the right. Why? Because here you are beginning to teach the left to right sequence we use in reading. Tell your child that this one (point to the biggest one) is bigger than this one (point to the smallest). Then point to the medium-sized toy and say it is bigger than this one (the small toy). Use other objects such as potatoes for dinner. Choose three different sizes and say, "Let's see, who shall get the big one?" "Who gets the little one?" Continue big and little using pots and pans. Show that the little one will fit into the big one, but not vice versa.

The more-less terminology is more difficult to teach because of stages in the child's mental development. These stages were clearly defined for us by a Swiss psychologist who showed that children can often be confused by how objects are physically arranged and how they see them as more or less. The big-little experiences may help set the stage for the more-less terminology but it is well to avoid making any major effort to teach the terminology.

COUNTING—AGAIN

The earlier discussion on counting related to your child in the years between one and one-half and three years. This discussion will focus on the three- and four-year-old.

Remembering the three types of counting, we now want to work on the second and third type. The second type was the one-to-one correspondence and the third type was the inclusiveness of the last numeral said by the child. Our goal is to develop these two skills.

Get out your sack of potatoes and place about four of them in a row. Have a pan to hold the potatoes. Say, "Can you say your numerals for me?" The child will generally be happy to show his or her ability. Say, "Now, let's learn to count potatoes. When you say a numeral I want you to put a potato in the pan. O.K., let's go." Here you have the child start from the left and as each potato is picked up and placed in the pan say, "How many potatoes are in the pan?" If you get a correct response say, with enthusiasm, "Right!" Quit here. If you get an incorrect response, say, "There are four potatoes in the pan." Nothing more. These lessons should last no more than five minutes. Do not think you have to stay with it until you have the correct response. We cannot emphasize that last statement too strongly.

At the next lesson tell the child you're going to play a game called "Can't peek." The idea of the game is to not look, but to count the potatoes. Have the four potatoes in the pan again. Have your child close his or her eyes and reach into the pan and take out a potato and say the numeral for each potato as it is removed from the pan. If your child has a little difficulty starting the procedure simply take his or her hand and grasp one potato and say, "One." Place the potatoes in a line as each one is removed. When the last one is removed, say, "Don't peek, how many potatoes were in the pan?" You know what to do if the child is right or wrong. If your child is picking this up quickly you can ask him or her to put a quantity of potatoes in the pan for you to count. Close your eyes as he or she puts them in the pan. Count them out. When finished counting say, "There were (quantity) potatoes in the pan. Am I right?"

Repeat these activities adding additional potatoes or blocks as time goes on until you reach the quantity of ten potatoes.

When the one-to-one correspondence and the inclusiveness of the last numeral verbalized is well established in your child's mind, you can ask him or her to give you a certain quantity from the sack of potatoes. "Can you get me five potatoes, please?" If your child should have difficulty with this task merely help him or her count them out. At the next lesson you will need to repeat the request and say, "How many potatoes do we want?" He or she should reply, "Five." "O.K.," you say, "We need to stop counting when we get to five. Please give me five potatoes."

In the chapter on the primary grades it is emphasized that you should not try formal teaching of your child but that you should provide many different experiences which will provide a readiness for formal instruction in the school years. This is not a lack of consistency in our philosophy; rather, we know there are certain learnings that must be given formal attention or else their acquisition will be extremely slow and incidental in coming, or left entirely until the school years.

SYMBOLS THAT SAY NUMBERS

A numeral is the correct word for the symbol we use to indicate a quantity we call number. In our culture you rarely hear people refer to the numeral six. Generally, they will say the number six, but numeral is correct when they mean the symbolic representation of a quantity.

When you want to assist your child in learning the numerals after the three types of counting have been learned, you could start by taking him or her outside and pointing to the house number. Ask, "Do you know what this is? It is our house number. It helps people find our house. See this? (Point to a numeral.) This is a (whatever numeral it is)." "Let's go inside and I will show you all the numerals you will ever need."

At this point you can present a chart you have constructed containing the following numerals: 0, 1, 2, 3, 4, 5, 6, 7, 8, 9, 10. The numerals should be large enough for the child to see from a distance of several feet. Once the chart is placed in a prominent spot in the child's room, do a quick run-through verbally. "This is a zero, next is a one, two," etc. At the next session say to your child, "Will you count to ten for me as I point to the numerals?" Then, "Now I'll count to ten and you point to the numerals." After this quick session and at the next one say, "Let's look at the way the numerals are formed." Here you should have prepared a large sheet of butcher paper, glossy side up. (This really is the kind of paper butchers use and not the unglazed paper one can buy in an art supply store.) Onto this paper you pour a batch of chocolate pudding. Smear it around. Say to your child, "Now, let's do some finger painting and make the numerals." Here you start off with your finger making the numeral one. As you do it say, "One is a straight line. Start at the top and come down. Numeral two is a curved line starting at the top, curve right, curve left, and end up with a flat line on the bottom. Three is two curves. Start at the top, curve right, curve left, and curve right again." Go through the numerals but before you complete them have your child start in on the process. Take his or her hand, pointed finger, and guide the repetition of the numerals. At a later session go back

54

outside and ask your child to say the numerals in your house number, those on the neighbor's house, etc. Be aware that some manufacturers have taken artistic license with numeral shapes. Therefore, you should decide if the activity will confuse your child rather than help him or her. Try the numerals on your car license number.

The final episode in the learning sequence should be for you to say a numeral and for your child to be able to point to it or hand it to you. For example, if you write each numeral on separate three-inch-by-five-inch index cards you can array them in front of your child and he or she can place them in order, pick up one you name, and so forth.

BABES IN COMPUTERLAND

With the coming of the reasonably priced home computer, so also has come the early learning programs in mathematics for preschoolers.

These programs are not a substitute for parental involvement in developing a familiarity with objects, numbers, and numeral concepts. Because the computer screen is the equivalent of paper and pencil exercises given in school, their level of abstraction is greater than having the child actually manipulate objects. Therefore, it is essential to have the child learn the concept of number and then, when the concept of number is mastered, proceed to the abstraction of numeral.

In considering programs for your preschooler you should preview before you purchase. Some of the elements you should consider are: Does the program reinforce the child's interest through some response mechanism? That is, does it have sound, color, musical tone? If an error is made in the child's response, is the response other than insulting? For example, a relatively friendly response is no response to an error; the child cannot move forward. An unfriendly response might be an unpleasant sound, a sad face flashed on the screen, etc. Another question would be, does the program move forward in small enough steps to be instructional yet not so slowly as to be boring? Are the characters recognizable to a small child? Does the program help the child develop a correct response if an error was made?

One example of some of the foregoing is in an activity where a preschooler is to match shapes. This is strictly a shape recognition activity. The computer provides no terminology. In this activity four shapes appear on the screen. They are numbered. One shape appears to the right of the screen. The child presses the key which has the same numeral as the appropriate shape on the left. Regardless of which numeral has been selected, the shape on the right will move over to the correct shape on the left. However, if the child has pressed the correct numeral, both shapes will begin to flash and a musical note will be heard. If the child was in error, a "uh-oh" sound is heard. The child may now try again.

This above illustration contains a number of the elements of a good program. It is self-instructional, it has sound, color, and reinforces a correct answer. However, it is not quite as friendly as it might be.

We do not urge you to rush out and buy a computer. If you have one, you might consider the possibility of buying some programs with which to reinforce your preschooler's learning of shapes, number, numeral.

SUMMARY

In this chapter we have urged you to begin the first steps to help your child achieve a readiness for the many learnings in arithmetic which will take place in the early grades. We have suggested some direct teaching activities which must be undertaken in order for your child to experience a sense of number and numeral. As we end this chapter we want to once again reinforce the ideas that the activities in which you and your child engage must be happy ones. They must not be tension filled. There is no one who is more important to the child than you, the parent. The child's sense of self-worth is established by your interaction with him or her. In our efforts to help our children achieve success let's not destroy both the sense of self-worth and what should be a love for understanding the mathematical world.

Finally, remember it is the concrete, hands-on experiences the child has that will lead to a successful grasp of the abstract manipulations of symbols that we call mathematics.

PART THREE

A Good Start: The Primary Grades

CHAPTER 5 Reading

Parents, teachers, and students are all a part of the educational process. Remove one part and reading education will not prosper as it should.

SINCE THE PARENTS stand out as a vital influence in the reading achievement of children in the primary grades, it is of extreme importance that parents know all they possibly can about the reading process in order to help their children develop in this most important act. In the primary grades your child learns to read. During the rest of his or her life your child reads to learn. Therefore, the primary grades become very important years for reading instruction. In this chapter, you will learn how to extend your child's interest in reading, how to assist in vocabulary development and word attack skills, as well as how to work with your child to help him or her in reading comprehension.

EXTENDING INTEREST

Parents need to foster positive attitudes toward reading. Many of the activities that you read in Chapter 2 regarding reading readiness will help in the primary grade years as well. Your child will still enjoy you reading to him or her.

Oral Reading

First grader Kendal came home from school with his preprimer book to read to his parents as requested by the teacher. The great amount of attention and praise that he got from his parents was quite disconcerting for his younger sister, Janae. She decided that if she were to get back into the spotlight with her parents, she needed to learn to read, and learn to read as quickly as possible. She observed her brother carefully as he pointed to each word as he read the line of print. She finally said, "You read with your finger don't you?" Kendal replied, "No silly, you read with your mouth." Oral reading is not always perceived by children in the proper way; however, oral reading is an excellent process for extending interest in reading for children.

As your child begins to learn how to read, he or she may take a more active role while you are reading aloud to him or her. You can now involve your child in the reading of the story by letting your child read certain words that he or she knows from each page. This activity of filling in the words from time to time is an excellent way to involve your child in oral reading. If the material being read has refrains where lines of print are repeated, you may have your child read the repeated material. The reading of plays written for children can be another exciting way to develop interest in reading and get your child to interact more in the reading process. Your child can take one or more character parts and you can take the other parts. Each one then would read the character parts as designated in the play.

Pointing to the words as you are reading is also helpful. This visually reinforces the word for your child and gives him or her an opportunity to see and hear the word simultaneously.

Oral reading during the primary grades can also be the time when you read books that are too difficult for your child to read alone. Thus, you extend interest to more difficult reading levels to keep your child's interest in reading during the time when he or she is laboring to learn to read simple materials.

Your child can now read books to you for oral reading activities. It is fun for your child to be able to read to you! Even the easiest preprimer books brought from school are exciting for him to read. This type of oral reading activity always helps your child keep interested in reading.

Large Supply of Books

It cannot be overemphasized that a large supply of books in your home is essential to help your child extend his or her interest in reading. These books can be the personal property of your child or they can be books borrowed from the public or school library. Going to the library is an excellent way to extend the interest in reading for your child. One of the best ways to develop positive attitudes toward reading is to give your child an opportunity not only to read an exciting book but to select it as well. Children of all ages should be able to have some part in the selection of the books that they wish to read because of the effect it has on developing positive feelings toward reading. Some parents may feel that their children will select books that are too difficult for them to read. It has been found that given a selection of many different kinds of books and reading levels, the child will usually select the book that fits his or her reading level. If this is not the case after several trips to the library, then you will need to guide your child in the selection of books that do fit his or her reading abilities. You may select several books that are at his or her reading level and ask your child to choose one of these books. Books and reading materials of all different kinds are an essential part of extending interest in reading for your child.

Books that have moving parts can serve as another approach for extending the reading interest for your child. These books, which are commonly called "pop up books," "peek-a-books," or "movable books," are quite popular with primary grade children and are an excellent source for motivating your child in reading. It has also been determined that these books help the child understand symbolic representations of words because of the three-dimensional effect these movable parts depict.

VOCABULARY DEVELOPMENT

As your child begins to attach concepts and ideas to vocabulary words as printed symbols in books, he or she is beginning the reading process. The vocabulary words your child acquires and will need in the reading process can be roughly divided into two categories, concrete and abstract words.

Concrete Vocabulary Words

Concrete vocabulary words, as contrasted with abstract vocabulary words, are usually easier for your child to understand. Concrete vocabulary words are made up of many nouns, pronouns, action verbs, and descriptive words. Nouns that your child sees as labels on cereal boxes, crayons, and soft drinks are concrete vocabulary words that your child associates with the actual object. Names of persons, places, and animals are easily identified with concrete words. Action verbs such as run, walk, jump, etc. are concrete words too. Descriptive words such as blue and green, and concept words such as big or little, are all concrete words with which your child usually will have no difficulty. Vocabulary words that are easily identified with the actual person, place, thing, action, or description are simpler for your child to understand and apply in the reading process.

To help your child work with concrete vocabulary words in the initial stages of reading, you can point out picture clues in the reading material that will assist your child in identifying the word. For example, while reading the sentence, "The ball is red," your child may be having difficulty with the word "ball" or "red." By looking at the picture clues, it is readily apparent that there is a ball in the picture and it is a red color. A picture dictionary is also very helpful for your child in identifying concrete words. The picture dictionary has concrete words listed with pictures by each word for identification. These picture dictionaries are available at bookstores and may be checked out of the school or public library for your child to use.

As your child matures in the reading process, the best way for increasing vocabulary words is through wide reading, thus using the vocabulary words in many different types of contextual reading settings.

Abstract Vocabulary Words

Six-year-old Debra asked, "When will I get to go to the movie?" Her mother replied, "Tomorrow." Debra asked again, "What is tomorrow?" Her mother replied, "The day after today is tomorrow." "Is today, tomorrow?" she queried again. This could go on for some time, because the word "tomorrow" is so abstract and hard for the six-year-old child to understand.

Abstract vocabulary words are very difficult because they have very little or no pictorial representation in one's mind like concrete vocabulary words do. Words like *these, those, when,* and *where* are but a few abstract words that cause difficulty in understanding; and yet, many of these words are introduced in some reading programs in the early part of first grade. With these words, meaning comes only when these words are attached to other words in phrases or sentences, for example, *these* apples, *when* will you go. In working with your child in developing his or her abstract vocabulary words, the best method for you to use is to put them into a phrase or sentence so that your child will be able to understand the usage of these words in a contextual setting. As with concrete words, abstract words are best understood as your child reads widely.

WORD ATTACK

The skills needed for decoding a word are called word attack. Word-attack skills are taught in school; however, many children learn certain techniques for word attack on their own. As some children learn word-attack skills on their own, they may develop some wrong generalizations. That is why it is essential that a good word-attack program be developed to aid children in this important aspect of reading. The four commonly used approaches for word attack in schools are phonics, contextual clues, structural analysis, and the use of sight words. Again, it is important to emphasize that this book is *not* intended to make you, the parent, into a teacher. It is necessary that you do know some *dos* and *don'ts* about word attack so that you will be able to assist your child in reading, not as a teacher, but as a concerned and interested parent.

Phonics

Do *not* teach your child phonics; let the school teacher do this. So often children are brought to the university reading clinic by highly interested parents. Their first comment most often is: "All my child needs is some training in phonics and then he or she will be able to read." Many times this is exactly what their child does not need. The parents have drilled their child in letter phonics so that he or she can go through the alphabet and give the sound of each letter. Sometimes the sound the child makes is so distorted that the child cannot put the sounds together to form a word, or the training in phonics is so overdone that the child spends all of his time in sounding out words and loses the real intent of reading, which is understanding.

There are many different methods of teaching phonics. The one that is being used by your child's teacher may not be the one with which you are familiar or the one that you learned when you were a child. You should not plan to teach your child phonics because it may confuse him or her by introducing another method of learning phonics skills.

The best way to help your child in phonics is to pronounce the difficult words for him or her. Don't exaggerate the sounds of the word as you say it but say it in a normal, conventional way. This will not only reduce frustrations for both of you, but it will keep the reading moving along and help tremendously in the understanding of what is being read.

Contextual Clues

Context is a normal and natural way to learn word attack. Words usually have their meaning only as they are found in context. As you are working with your child in reading and he or she comes to a word that is unknown, have your child skip over the unknown word and read the rest of the sentence. After completing the sentence, ask your child to now go back to that word and see if he or she can figure out the word from the contextual clues given in the sentence. Usually the child can say the word after reading the contextual clues in the sentence.

Words that are spelled in a similar way but pronounced differently can cause difficulty for children. For example the word *tear* is pronounced differently depending on how it is used. Look at the following two sentences:

The boy had a *tear* in his eye.

Please *tear* the paper into four equal pieces.

Only by seeing the word in context can one determine how to pronounce it. As your child reads and comes across words that are spelled alike but can be pronounced differently, let him or her read to the end of the sentence even if he or she pronounced it incorrectly, and then bring the incorrectly pronounced word to your child's attention. Through contextual clues, help your child determine how that word should be pronounced.

Structural Analysis

Structual analysis is used to identify a word through the analysis of the basic parts of that word. Prefixes, suffixes, inflectional endings, syllabication, and compound words are the categories of structural analysis. Whereas in phonics, one attacks words through an aural approach, a student uses his or her visual sense in structural analysis.

As prefixes come at the beginning of the word and are often very simple to pronounce, they usually do not cause your child difficulty in attacking and pronouncing them. The problem here is usually one of understanding what the prefix does to the root word in changing its meaning. It is usually more important to stress meaning rather than word attack when working with prefixes. Some common prefixes and their meanings are listed to give you an example of what the prefixes do to the root words.

Prefix	Meaning	Example
in-	not	incorrect
un-	not	unafraid
	opposite of	untie
dis-	not	dislike
re-	again	reread
	back	refund
mis-	wrong, bad	mistreat
pre-	before	predict

A simple, easily read prefix can certainly alter the meaning of a sentence. It is important for you to help your child understand the meaning of the common prefixes and to help him or her see what happens to the meaning of the root word when prefixes are used. It will definitely affect your child's comprehension if he or she does not pay attention to the prefixes in words.

Suffixes and inflectional endings are added to the end of the root word and usually cause some difficulty for the reader. Unlike prefixes that change the meaning of the root word, suffixes and inflectional endings usually change the usage of the word in the sentence or change the tense, number, or degree of the word. Many times the suffixes and inflectional endings also change the spelling of the word and this may cause some difficulty for your child in reading or identifying the word because its root has been changed to a different spelling. The best way you can help your child in this area is to be available to help him or her as he or she encounters words with these endings. It is better to tell your child the word, than to get into a lengthy discussion of why the word is as it is. On occasion you may point out what the root word is in the word that gives your child difficulty and supply for your child the correct spelling of the root word, if necessary,

Dividing a word into smaller parts for attacking the word is known as syllabication. The usual purpose for dividing the word is to allow your child to attack smaller parts of the word, thus enabling him or her to put the parts together to form a word. Many rules have been developed for syllabication, but it is not necessary for you to get involved in going over the rules with your child. If an assignment comes home from school concerning syllabication and your child has some difficulty with certain words, you can teach your child to use the dictionary or you can help him or her in finding the problem words. Most dictionaries have the words divided into syllables; therefore, you will not need to worry about knowing the rules.

Compound words are usually quite easy for your child to decode because a compound word has two or more smaller words within the larger word. Your child can deal with the smaller words and put them together in order to pronounce the larger word. If your child needs assistance, you can help by pointing out the smaller words within the larger word and if necessary help him or her to pronounce the word.

Sight Words

Sight words are of two types. One type of sight word is a word that is used over and over again by the reader until that word is so familiar that it becomes part of his or her sight vocabulary. This type of sight word is what makes up most of your reading vocabulary as an adult, but because your child is not mature in reading, he or she will have a very limited sight vocabulary. The second type of sight word is a word that cannot be determined through one of the methods of word attack mentioned above. For example, the word *was* is a sight word that fits the second type. It is a phonetically irregular word and is learned by your child through repetition until he or she learns how to do it without help.

To increase your child's sight word vocabulary of the first type all you need to do is to give your child many opportunities for wide reading. It is through wide reading that your child will enlarge his or her sight vocabulary. To help your child with sight word problems of the second type, pronounce the word for your child when he or she cannot determine how the word should be pronounced.

COMPREHENSION

Kathleen, who was in the third grade, was reading orally for her teacher. She was doing very well in pronouncing each word perfectly, pausing at the commas, stopping at each period, and using her voice to give emphasis where needed. After completing the reading assignment, her teacher took the book from Kathleen's hands, and asked, "Tell me, Kathleen, what was happening to the main character in this story?" Kathleen replied, "I wasn't listening." Indeed, Kathleen was probably not thinking about what she was reading. It is important to remember that reading is an active thinking process and requires the reader to be involved in the story so comprehension can take place. Even though a child may say all the words as Kathleen did, the reader must have understanding in order for reading to actually take place.

Comprehension is what reading is all about. If one calls out the words but does not understand what he or she is reading, then that is more appropriately labeled as "word calling" rather than reading. Reading requires that a purpose be established for reading the passage. This purpose will direct the reader and help him or her to read for understanding in order to find that purpose. Some of the major purposes for comprehension in the primary grades are understanding word meanings, drawing inferences, and locating answers.

Word Meanings

The first aspect of comprehension is the ability to understand the meaning of each word read. It is helpful if your child understands the meaning of isolated words, but word meaning depends upon the context in which the word is found. The best way to help your child is to assist him or her in understanding the meaning of the word as it appears in the reading material. This can be done by giving your child a synonym or antonym of the word that he or she is having some difficulty understanding. You may also help your child in the use of a dictionary to help him or her discover the meaning of certain words. The ideas given earlier in this chapter, in the word attack area, will also help you here in word meanings, especially those suggestions found in contextual clues and structural analysis sections.

Questioning Techniques

To help your child with comprehension, you can ask questions concerning the reading done by your child. You need to ask questions to get your child to recall details and main ideas that are directly stated in the reading material. This can be done by you as you quickly glance over the material your child has read silently and then ask questions concerning details and/or main ideas. If he or she is reading orally, you need to listen to the oral reading and then ask questions concerning details and main ideas. These questions do not have to be elaborate or extensive, only enough questioning needs to take place to make sure your child is understanding what he or she is reading.

Locating Answers

Children have difficulty in finding the answers to questions posed in their reading assignment. Many times this is because they do not fully understand the question. If your child needs help in this area, you need to first learn if your child actually understands the question. This can be done by asking your child what the questions are actually asking him or her to find. Get your child to paraphrase the question in his or her own words. Many times children will give back to you the question verbatim as written in the book still not understanding the words; therefore, paraphrasing is important because it will cause your child to at least understand the idea well enough to put it into his or her own words. If your child cannot do this, you will need to paraphrase the question yourself so that your child understands it. After understanding the question, usually your child will not have difficulty finding the answer.

If your child does understand the question, but cannot find the answer, you will need to redirect your child's reading to certain paragraphs that have the answer. Do not give him the answer, but direct him or her to reread the paragraph that contains the answer and let him or her find the answer through a second, more thorough reading.

Because comprehension is the end product of reading, you will find your child spending a great amount of time in school developing comprehension skills. You must continue to encourage him or her to read for understanding even if this means to read the passage all over again. Comprehension is an active thinking process and you need to encourage your child to be involved in his or her reading. Establishing a purpose for reading will help make it an active thinking process. You should help your child to establish a purpose so he or she will read for details, main ideas, and to find answers to questions asked.

SUMMARY

Reading in the primary grades is an essential developmental task that your child needs to learn. Encouragement is needed in any school activity; however, in the area of reading, encouragement is absolutely necessary. It is a complex task, yet most children do learn to read and your child will too!

Your best effort in helping your child in reading is through your ability to foster positive attitudes toward reading. Spend your time in being a good model by reading yourself and enjoying the reading that you do. Encourage your child to read for recreation and enjoyment as well.

Be pleased to be a part of the educational process for, after all, what is more important than assisting your child to be a success in school. A little effort now will certainly reap big dividends for your child in the future. Remember the statement: Children learn to read in the primary grades and for the rest of their lives they read to learn.

CHAPTER 6 Writing

For primary children, writing develops from invention to modeling. Their awkward yet fascinating attempts offer glimpses into creative, complex, and caring young minds.

EARLY IN THE first-grade year, a six-year-old child wrote the story on page 74. Unlike the "hostage" story in Chapter 3, this story is a bit easier for us to read. It also has several words that are spelled correctly. But notice also that the word "the" is spelled correctly in the title and spelled "thy" (pronounced "thee") at the end of the story. Such variability is common at this stage and, together with obvious "invented" spellings, is to be expected when children are focusing on *meaning* in their writing.

As your child begins school, you may wonder about whether this "playful" approach to written language should now be eased into the background and a more "serious" attitude assumed. Resist this temptation. Children should be allowed to continue to produce writing without warnings from us about proper spelling, complete sentences, and so forth. Home should be the one place where your child is free to experiment with and to enjoy spoken and written language.

The influence of school is of course going to be evident in a number of ways in your child's writing during the first three grades. You will notice some intriguing changes in both the appearance and the content of this writing. It is common for most

THE STORYA BAOT A
OCHRG THAT LOSTAFATHR

OIN DAY A OCHRG LOST
A FATHR CHYWISSO AER
CHY STAPT HR FYTO.
AND CHY PICTETAPCHY
CHRIYD TO POTITON
CHYCOD NOT POTI TON
WIN CHY WOCAP THE
NACSTMOANYN CHY FAN
AATHR FTHR THYINO

children to go through "spurts" of writing in a particular form. Do not be worried if you observe that your child does not seem to be writing as much this week as last. He or she may indeed still be writing, but in a different style. Stories may not be popular for a while, but you may notice that lists, directions and instructions, labels, and perhaps a newspaper are being produced. Rules for

74

club membership—for example, a written "test" for admission to a club—qualify as writing and serve quite nicely as vehicles through which writing competence develops.

Before getting down to *your* role in your child's writing, let's consider some different compositions of children in grades one through three in order to get a "feel" for the directions your child's writing may take.

Early in the first grade a child was entranced by a diagram in one of his parents' books. The diagram was of the human body, alongside of which several of the more important organs were

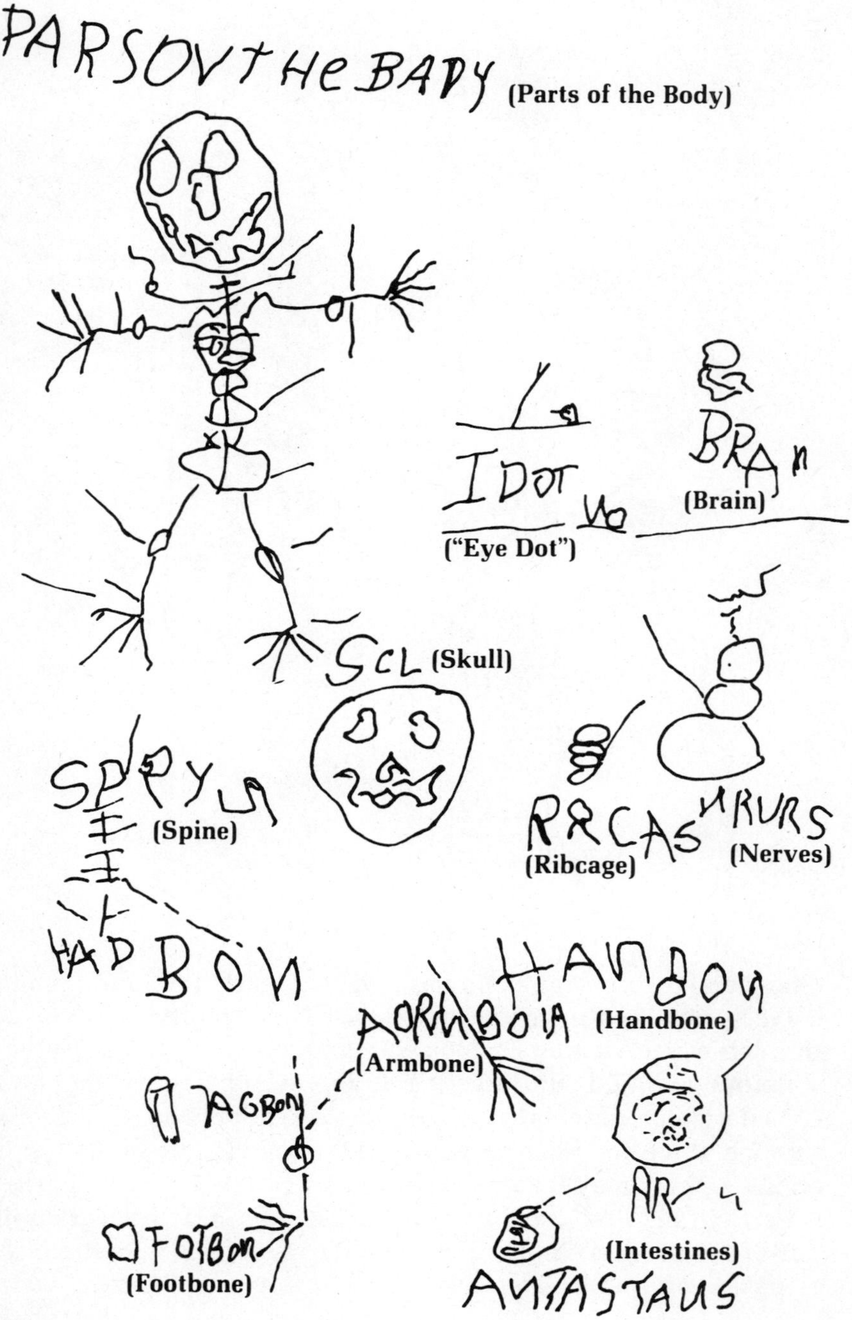

PARSOVTHeBADY (Parts of the Body)

I DOT ("Eye Dot")

BRA n (Brain)

SCL (Skull)

SPPYL∩ (Spine)

RRCAS (Ribcage) MRURS (Nerves)

HADBON

HANDON (Handbone)

AORMBOIA (Armbone)

AGBON

FOTBON (Footbone)

ARL∩ (Intestines)

AUTASTAUS

76

separately illustrated and labeled. The child drew his own diagram, "Parts of the Body." In addition to "sounding out" the
spelling of the parts, this child exhibited a delightful bit of creative thinking by labeling the pupil of the eye "eye dot." He did not
know the name of that part of the eye, so he aptly described it!
This "diagram" is an excellent example of many beginning first
graders' invented spellings, and it demonstrates how capable
children are of generating purposeful, meaningful written pro-
ductions.

The following story, written by a first grader in the second
month of the school year, illustrates more invented spelling but
also reveals a child who is using writing to deal with his own
"monsters"—real as well as metaphorical:

MOSTRS

w^ons a pona time thir wis a mosr he wis a men,
won he wod chaes pepol in haoses and
in the poarc too wet a tar mostrshe wiss
thin a athr bot cam fil iv mostrs
thay did the sam tha

won mostr cot a child named david thy

at him up for sipr

%5 won boy smortr thn the mostrs

he sol a mostr thin he aet the
mostr up for his sapr
thin he sal the hol g p

he at thm for picfist the nacst

mornen

the ind

(Once upon a time there was a monster. He was a mean one.
He would chase people in houses and in the park, too. What a
terrible monster he was. Then another bunch came full of
monsters. They did the same thing.
One monster caught a child named David. They ate him up for supper.
One boy, smarter than the monsters, he saw a monster then he ate
the monster up for his supper. Then he saw the whole group.
He ate them for breakfast the next morning.

The End)

BACK TO BASICS

As the story attests, writing can be very therapeutic—even for a youngster!

The following letter by a second grader is also therapeutic in a way, but also represents a touching attempt to "make amends" with a parent who was obviously quite irate about something—and who was in no mood to discuss the matter with his son!

```
                    Dear daddy,

                        I promes I will peck up well too

            night.  On the weekends I will help out.  I
            allwase try to help out, but sumtimes I gofe.

            Can we buy icecreme after denner?

            I was not tring to say that you were mad at

            me I was only tring to apolageise to you.
            You know that I love you very much!  I want

            thank you for leting me yose the tiperiter.

            If we can't buy icecreme let's

        pop popcorn.  I watcht little house on the prary.

                                    I love you,
```

This child is not only learning to write, but is using writing as a vehicle for exploring and for expressing some very deep interpersonal concerns. Such little notes remind us that, for a number of reasons, *talking* may not always be the best way to communicate.

Quite often writing does it better, and leaves a more lasting impression on both the writer and the reader.

A third grader wrote the following introduction and "score summary sheet" for a test. Notably, the test was never written!

```
                    TESTING!

        WE ARE GOING   TO   TEST YOU   TO   SEE

        IIF YOU CAN BE   IN THE GANG.
          IF YOU PASS  THE  TEST YOU WILL

        OFCOURSE YOU WIL BE IN THE GANG,

        BUT IF YOU FAIL THE TEST ████

          DON'T FEEL SORRY YOU STILL WILL
        PROBLEY DO GOOD.  GOOD LUCK!

        ━━━━━━━━━━━━━━━
             N.R.A. STAGE G.  (GANG )
```

```
        NAMES           SCORE  ‖   ‖   ‖   ‖
        MATT           ====‖===‖==‖==‖==
                       ====‖===‖==‖==‖==
        R ICKEY        ====‖===‖==‖==‖==
                       ====‖===■==‖==‖==
                       ===‖===‖==‖==‖==
        LARRY          ==‖==_‖==‖==‖==
                       ====‖===‖==‖==‖==
        JASON          ====‖===‖==‖==‖==
                       ===‖====‖==‖==‖==
        KEVIN          ===‖===‖==‖==‖==
                         ‖
```

BACK TO BASICS

As we've noted, writing serves many purposes. Children spend much time and effort planning for and organizing clubs. Such was the case here. Whatever "gang" was being organized was short-lived, but the prospect of organizing the gang was exciting enough to generate this composition. Children give back to us in their writing what they experience in their reading. Third graders know a lot about tests! Although this composition is modeled on a test format, one is struck by the sensitivity of the young writer to the test-taker (perhaps a reflection of the writer's experience with a test?): "But if you fail the test don't feel sorry you still will probably do good. Good luck!"

When children are free to write, they reveal to us some fascinating, humorous, and occasionally sobering thoughts. If you can serve as a means of facilitation and support, you may gain as much from your child's learning experience as he or she does.

HELP YOUR CHILD KEEP THE WRITING GOING

In Chaper 3 we talked about how your child can "invent" his or her own spellings. Armed with a knowledge of the letters of the alphabet, he or she will be able to write whatever needs to be said. We also pointed out that, far from instilling poor spelling habits, this type of strategy "pays off" in the long run in more creative writing and also better spelling. You should continue to encourage these inventions as your child begins the primary grades. Rest assured that this encouragement is perhaps the soundest support you can give with the "how to" of writing at this stage.

There comes the day when, if your child has been coming up with his or her own spelling in his stories, he or she will probably ask you if certain words are spelled right. We suggest the following type of response: "Julie, I really like how you sounded that word out. You'll see it spelled in books this way . . ." and then you can spell the word for the child. You have done two things with such a response; you have verbally rewarded the child for a good attempt and you have acknowledged that words are spelled a certain way in books. For most children, this type of attitude on the part of adults is enough to keep them going with their invented spelling—if an obliging adult is not around they can still write down what they wish to say. Importantly, however, we have not made a "big deal" about correct spelling.

YOU AND YOUR CHILD: TALKING, READING, AND THINKING

Your child's writing relies on experiences and on thinking about those experiences. Much of this thinking will be largely as a result of talking with you. Another most critical source for writing is of course the *reading* that your child does. When children are read to, and when they read themselves, they are not only provided with a sense of the *structure* of books, stories, and poems. Importantly, the *language* to which they are exposed works its way first into their subconscious and then out again, sometimes in eddies, other times in torrents. From our adult perspective its use is at first awkward and inappropriate, but as with all aspects of learning it must be tried out and exercised; only with use and experience will it achieve its more noble sense and cadence. As is noted in Chapter 2, when your child hears you read, particularly if it is the acknowledged "better" literature of our combined cultural heritage, then the words and phrasing of precise, appropriate, and eloquent language begin to become a part of your child's makeup. With time, these words and phrasings will help your child unlock subtle and insightful revelations about himself, the world, and his or her place in it. Such is the power of the language from books. And it is in *writing* where this subconscious stream of language will most likely be tapped and here it will begin to serve its role in affording powerful new thoughts and awarenesses.

As the above samples demonstrate, your child's writing can take many directions. Our purpose with the following suggestions is not to suggest how you may respond to all possible compositions from your child. Rather, we have chosen as illustrations some types of writing other than stories that children frequently have occasion to engage in.

BACK TO BASICS

THE WRITING PROCESS

For most individuals, compositions do not flow in perfect form from the pen. Rather, there is a *process* of writing in which the creating of a composition is broken down into four stages: prewriting, writing, revision, and proofreading. This partitioning of the writing process may surprise some who have thought that writing should somehow be "final" when it is put on the page. As writers, however, we do not think of everything we want to say and then simply put it on paper. We *do* plan and get the ideas going before writing, but we have every right to expect that our writing may go through many changes before we are satisfied with it. In addition, we have every right to expect that the finer points and niceties of proper grammar, sentence structure, and spelling need not overly preoccupy us during the early phases of our writing; rather, we can deal with them in the "revision" and proofreading stages. Your child should learn this attitude and this approach to writing.

THE FIRST REPORT

All four steps involved in the writing process may be handled informally beginning in second grade. In first grade there certainly can be prewriting—discussion about a topic and perhaps drawing an illustration—but revision and proofreading are usually not pursued with most children.

Prewriting

The first opportunity you may have to facilitate this more systematic approach to the writing process will be the day your second or third grader comes home and announces, "I have to write a report!" Although "report" writing does not usually begin in earnest until the upper elementary grades, it is not uncommon for children to begin to deal with them in the primary grades. They

82

need not be the full-blown report you probably remember writing in the upper elementary and middle school years, but they do represent a significantly different type of writing. And, it is certainly not uncommon for children to be uncertain just what a "report" exactly is! This should be established before any further thinking and writing are done.

Jerome, a second-grade acquaintance of ours, proudly announced one March afternoon that he had to write a report for the next day. When asked what the report was about, Jerome answered, "The sun." The conversation then went something as follows:

"Anything in particular about the sun?"

"Nope! Just the sun."

"Tell me, Jerome, what *is* a report?"

"I'm not sure. It tells you about stuff."

"That's just about it. It tells your reader *important* information about something. Well, let's try to come up with some ideas that we could write about having to do with the sun. Why do you think the sun is so important?"

"It gives light."

"Good! What else?"

"Hmmm . . . Oh! It keeps us warm, too!"

"Right again. What sorts of things need light and warmth?"

"Well, I guess *people* do, and animals."

"Do you suppose *plants* need light, too?"

"Oh, yeah!"

"Well, you've gotten a good start with your ideas for your report. Let's check the dictionary and see what it says about the sun." This provides a good check on ideas before the report is undertaken. It is an excellent idea for children to think about what they *know* about a topic before dealing with what they may *not* know. If many ideas are generated, write them down in a brief list so that they will be remembered. Of course, an encyclopedia could be consulted as well, but unless it is a set geared for youngsters, best to leave it alone for now. The same thing goes, by the way, for dictionaries. Jerome, however, had his own child's dictionary, and looked up the "s" section. He needed help to find the word at that point.

"Well, look here, Jerome. Read what it says next to the word 'sun.' "

" 'A star around which the planets and the earth revolve. It gives heat and light.' Hey! It says almost exactly what I said. But *this* is *weird!* It says the sun's a *star!* That's crazy!"

"Why is it crazy?"

"The sun's not a star—it's too big!"

Here the discussion will take an obvious turn. Jerome is going to experience a major restructuring of his concepts about stars and suns, and is likely to be significantly impressed by this new knowledge.

Writing

After the brief discussion—part of the "prewriting" stage—the child can set about the task of writing his "report." At this grade level, a one-paragraph production is usually acceptable.

"Jerome, you've got some good information to include in your report now. You can say *what* the sun is, and you can say *why* it's important. I wonder: Could you also say something about what might happen if we didn't *have* the sun?" You're of course providing another possibility here, but also, most importantly, you are modeling what is referred to as critical, divergent thinking—a highly significant and valuable tool.

> The sun is a star. It is the closest star to the earth. The sun gives the earth lite and it keeps the earth warm. These are things that all living things need to live on earth.
>
> If we didn't have the sun none of us would be alive. It would be very very cold and dark. I'm glad we have a friendly star so close to us!

Revising and Proofreading

Jerome was pleased with his "report," and didn't feel as though it should be changed. His parent did encourage him to read it over to make sure, since this would be the final copy to be handed in, that there were no spelling errors. Jerome didn't find any, so his parent pointed to "lite," and told Jerome, "You sounded this one out well, Jerome. Let's check the dictionary again and read what it says about the sun. We can notice how *they* spell the word light."

The parent could have also simply told Jerome the spelling. Because this was the only misspelling, however, Jerome would probably remember the spelling better if he took the short time to check it himself. It is wiser to strike a balance between providing immediate help and requiring the child to search actively for the spelling. We will pursue this issue a little further in the spelling and handwriting section below.

LETTER WRITING

We have the best of intentions. We know how much grandma and grandpa would treasure a letter from their grandchild so we suggest, encourage, and in some regrettable instances, coerce our child into writing one. Along with the genuine explanations of how much such a letter would mean to a grandparent—or other elderly relatives or acquaintances—we can provide more positive support by helping our children to list and organize whatever they might want to talk about.

Prewriting

This is *not* a step to make a big deal about. Simply help your child to identify the important things that grandma and grandpa would probably be interested in, and write them down. Just a word or two will suffice. Then, when the blank page is facing your child, he or she will be *ready* to write. This simple procedure is laying important groundwork for later on when your child will need to realize that he or she is communicating with a person who is not right there in front of them but who is removed in time and space.

85

BACK TO BASICS

This more "objective" stance is critical for successful learning and literacy experiences.

Writing

Once your child is writing about the "important points," other matters may occur to him or her. Encourage your child to jot them down so that they may be referred to later in the letter. Again, we are not concerned with a lengthy composition, but simply with the ideas expressed—at this age level, a sentence or two about each idea is usually the norm.

Revising and Proofreading

Unless the letter is intended for someone with whom your child is not familiar, a scratched-out misspelling and correction are fine. Simply suggest to your child that he or she read the letter over upon completion; this is an unobtrusive but valuable suggestion.

"FREE WRITING"

A popular technique by which students examine their thoughts through writing and which is used very effectively by teachers of English at both the elementary and secondary levels is the use of a "journal" by each student. At their simplest level, these journals may be merely a diary but, more often, are used as vehicles for children to express their thoughts about many different matters. At home, these can take the form of notebooks in which just about anything can be written down. Books that are set up and labeled as "My Diary," for example, often constrain children's writing and, if they are partitioned into specific calendar dates, do not have many lines for each day. It is better simply to have a notebook. When a diary-type entry is desired, fine; when any other type of entry is desired—"report" on snakes, reporter-style account of an incident, an essay on the ills of cafeteria food, and so forth—the notebook may be used as well.

The "Basics" Separately Considered: Spelling and Handwriting

If the orientation towards writing discussed here and in Chapter 9 is maintained, if your child reads, and if in school, words are examined carefully from a variety of perspectives, then yes, your child's knowledge of correct spelling is fairly well insured. And if your child values his or her piece of writing and expects that it will have an audience, then handwriting achieves a very important status indeed. The rudiments of effective handwriting—letter formation, paper orientation, holding the pen, and so forth—are taught in school; teachers work from a handwriting standard or model for the children. Your child will develop his or her own style, and as long as it is neat and legible in the "final" copy we should be pleased. The handwriting model in school should not be interpreted as a form of handwriting which children will imitate *exactly*. Rather, it is a standard that their writing will *approximate*.

The key factor is that the child's urge to write is not thwarted by a misplaced emphasis on proper letter formation. It is simply not true, despite the claims of some, that stylish and attractive handwriting is necessary for clear and well-reasoned writing. As with so much of writing, how legible our handwriting is depends on our purposes. A first draft may appear atrocious; the final draft which is to be posted on the bulletin board in the hallway should be legible and neat.

SUMMARY

We have seen that children can be surprisingly and delightfully creative in their written efforts in the primary grades. As parents, our task is to keep these natural efforts fun and, when appropriate, to facilitate the process by which these efforts can continue to develop. In this chapter, we have discussed the following:

1. As with the preschool child, the primary grade child needs to be engaged in discussion and exposed to reading. Importantly, the reading should be both by the child and by an adult *to* the child.

2. Continue to model how writing serves a *functional* purpose in your life. Talk about its purpose as you are engaged in it.

3. How to help your child come to appreciate and to follow the "writing process"—prewriting, writing, revising and proofreading. We have discussed some types of writing through which the process can be facilitated:

   The *"First Reports."* You will help your child appreciate how this type of writing helps him or her to identify what he or she knows about a topic and to obtain some additional information about that topic.

   Letters. Letters to loved ones and friends help your child during the "prewriting" stage to identify and organize what he or she wants to say. Letter writing will help your child in beginning the developmental process by which a sense of "audience" is developed—the reader is not immediately present but is removed in time and in space.

   Free writing. Encouraging this type of free writing helps your child to develop the excellent habit of writing down thoughts and observations on just about anything. Despite its simplicity, keeping a journal will help your child to "talk" to him or herself and to examine his or her thoughts more carefully.

4. Spelling and handwriting are important when attended to at the appropriate stage in the writing process. Your child will appreciate their value if they are seen as effective skills for clearly communicating to the reader the ideas expressed in the writing.

5. Keep it fun! Once again, you should not feel that you must become a constant teacher to your child. If you pursue the ideas suggested in this chapter, you will be facilitating a process (1) by which your child *thinks* before, during, and after writing, and (2) a process by which your child actually *writes*. In addition, you will be developing your child's positive attitude toward writing.

CHAPTER 7 Arithmetic

"Curiouser and curiouser!... how puzzling it
all is! Let me see: four times five times seven
is—oh dear! I shall never get to twenty at that
rate!"

—*Alice's Adventures in Wonderland and
Through the Looking Glass*. Lewis Carroll,
E. P. Dutton, Inc., 1865

THE PRIMARY GRADES are where your child develops his or her first
formal contacts with arithmetic. In the preschool chapter many
readiness activities were stressed and many concept-building activities were suggested. Now, your child will be encountering the
first direct instruction in arithmetic. This experience may be like
the mythical looking-glass world of Lewis Carroll's classic,
Alice's Adventure in Wonderland, referred to above.

It is here in the years of formal instruction that you can be a
warm, sensitive friend to your child as he or she encounters the
first experiences of evaluation by persons other than loving family members.

If your child experiences difficulty in understanding the arithmetic content in school you will be tempted to tutor, to teach, to
introduce new topics. This is a natural tendency but one you
should avoid. Instead, continue to work with your child in a non-
formal, interactive way. Provide multiple experiences on a daily,
casual basis. Use games and incidental activities to reinforce the
child's acquisition of concepts.

BACK TO BASICS

As a parent, you need to know what your child is expected to learn in each of the primary grades. If you have the total picture, you can better judge progress and work with your child in an informal and play-like manner. To acquaint you with the progression of arithmetic during the first three grades the authors will briefly outline the topics typically covered in each of the grades. Remember, these are only broad guidelines and are intended to be guides rather than absolutes for each grade.

FIRST GRADE

In the first grade, the teacher is trying to develop the ability to count and write the numerals zero through nine. The ideas of *more* and *less,* and of *sets* and *numbers* are introduced. The most elemental picture and bar graphs are generally discussed. The teacher will introduce the idea of zero in addition and subtraction. Vertical forms of addition and subtraction will be introduced. The teacher will introduce fractions in the most basic way: halves, one-half; thirds, one-third; fourths, one-fourth; time and money.

Depending upon the level of the class, the particular teacher, and the textbook used, the class may be introduced to sums thirteen through eighteen.

PARENTAL HELP

What can you do as a parent to help your child in the acquisition of so many topics? One thing is to make practical applications of arithmetic wherever you can. These practical applications can be at home, on the way to school, at the grocery store, or whenever you and your child encounter a situation that requires arithmetic in an understandable situation. Try to be sensitive to what the teacher is trying to teach at a particular point in time and reinforce it through practical, indirect activities. The following suggestions will be helpful and will suggest additional learning techniques.

On the way to the store, you might ask, "How many red lights do you think we'll get? Let's count them. You be the red light counter and hold up a finger each time we hit one." Upon arrival at the destination, you say, "How many fingers do you have up? Let's count together . . . one, two, three, etc." On the way home: "How many green lights . . ." "Did we get more green lights or red lights?" This last question may be difficult, because the child is still trying to learn one-to-one correspondence. Therefore, the more-less question could be too difficult. In that case, you might say, "Four is more than three. See?" Here, hold four of your child's fingers on one hand and three on the other.

Another example: "Mary, will you get me a set of four dishes, please?" or, "Mary, will you stack those four dishes, please."

"Let's count how many steps it is across the room." The child takes one step, and the parent says, "one," another step, "two," etc.

There is no substitute for lots of parent-child interaction in the development of children's arithmetic awareness. Whenever possible, explain what you are doing. Even if you are sorting nuts and bolts in the garage, say, "I'm putting all these nuts in one group and all these bolts in another. This is called a set of nuts and a set of bolts." As an adult, you may have forgotten that you classify things all the time. You do it unconsciously. However, the process is new to your child; and your help can be of great value in his understanding of these elementary mathematical operations.

When you sort the clothes for laundering, say: "Will you help me by making a pile of dark clothes and a pile of light ones?" When the task is completed, remember to compliment the child if the sorting process was done correctly. Then you might say, "Wash the set of light clothes first and then the set of dark ones." Notice the substitution of *set* for *pile*.

The reward system is useful both as an incentive and as a teaching method. When there is a chance to reward the child for activity, no matter how insignificant, try to reward him or her with a uniform type of coin—preferably pennies. Save them in a jar in the child's room. Count them periodically with your child as you both dump them on the floor and put the accumulation back in the jar. Later, when there are twenty-five or more, suggest that now might be a good time to spend them. Explain to your child that it is inconvenient to carry twenty-five pennies to the store—perhaps it would be a good idea to convert them into something easier to carry. Suggest that you will change them for nickels. Say that for every five pennies you can get one nickel. Have the child stack the pennies into sets of five each. Beside each set of five pennies, place a nickel. Then, go to the store and help your child purchase a twenty-five-cent object. Be aware that some children, depending upon their stage of development, may feel they are being cheated if you take five objects and only give them one in return. The exchange of five for one must often be taken on faith. If the child objects to the exchange, don't force it. Merely accept his or her objection, and take the twenty-five pennies to the store. You will at least have provided an awareness, so that when it is introduced in school, the child will remember the episode and be able to accept the concept more readily.

If you have stairs anywhere in your home, start the chant:

> Fireman, fireman, we can't wait;
> There's a fire in apartment Eight.
> Up the stairs he'll drag the hose;
> Count the steps as up he goes—
> 1, 2, 3, 4, 5, 6, 7, 8, 9, 10.

Do the chant before you take the first step; then, loudly stomp up each step, counting as you go.

In order to learn addition, the typical teaching pattern is to have children count items in a set, combine the set, and count the total set.

You may proceed in various ways to help your child acquire this concept. One way is to construct a number line on the carpet. Remember when you counted the steps across the room? This time, take one- or two-inch-wide masking tape and stretch it across the room on the carpet. At equal intervals of approximately a foot, draw the appropriate numeral. Suggest to your child that you play a bedtime card game together. When the child reaches the doorway, the game is over; and it's off to bed.

Remove the face cards and aces from a deck of cards. Eliminate two of the suits, leaving one of each color remaining. Tell your child that a black card moves him forward and the red ones indicate a backward move. It's a good idea to remove all red cards with a value over five, or bedtime may never come! Array the cards as a fan in your hand. With much fanfare (no pun intended) say, "Pick a card, any card!" The child then picks a card and executes the number of steps indicated. Then it is time to pick again. Ultimately, a red card will be encountered. For these, the child backs up the appropriate number of steps. When the child has advanced the first series of steps and has just picked the next card, say, "Six steps and (the next card) four steps is how many steps?" The child moves forward four more steps and lands on the numeral ten. The same activity is done in reverse when a red card is drawn: "Five steps take away three steps is. . . ."

During the above activity, be sure to count with the child as each step in a series is executed. In this way, the counting procedure is reinforced.

Zero is a legitimate number and is used to describe the empty set. "What is the number of elephants in this room?" "Zero," you respond if the child does not provide the word. Work with your child in understanding the zero concept. "On the rug by the foot of the bed, put all of your fire engines" (or whatever toy you know your child does not have). "I don't have any," your child replies. "The number that describes that is zero," you respond.

A simple subtraction activity that can be done at the kitchen table is to give your child no more than nine beans, peas, etc. Using a plastic cup, say, "Put your beans in a row." Hide two of them (cover with a cup) and say, "Nine beans . . . take away two is . . . seven." Do an inverse operation, such as, "Two beans plus (add) five beans is . . . seven."

Fractions

In the first grade, it is usually sufficient to learn the concept of halves, thirds, and fourths and the terms one-half, one-third, and one-fourth.

93

BACK TO BASICS

These terms and concepts are understood most successfully at the primary grades through the use of practical experiences. This is true with many mathematical concepts.

When you unwrap a candy bar, ask, "Would you like half?" Assuming an affirmative answer, make a real show of getting the bar cut into two equal lengths. Ask, "Are they the same? O.K., you have one-half, and I have one-half."

If you order pizza, ask, "If we were to cut this pizza into equal parts so that you and I have the same amount, where should I cut it?" In developing the concepts of fourths, however, you could say, "What if there were you, me, and two of your friends here, and we wanted to each have the same amount? How would you cut the pizza?"

In working with thirds, watch for an opportunity to find a pre-marked natural object. For example, a chocolate bar may already be divided into sections. Break apart a segment with three squares. Then you may explain, "Oh, look. I broke this into one-third segments. See . . . one, two, three."

Another opportunity involves asking your child to sweep a designated portion of the sidewalk. Say, "Would you mind sweeping from here to here? Oh, notice that each segment of the part you have to sweep is one-third."

By watching for object lessons in all situations, we can find opportunities to give practical experiences with fractions. Please remember to make all the situations fun and to praise sincerely for things done well and done correctly.

SUMMARY

It is important to reiterate that the work you do with your child must be low in tension. It should be a game or activity. It should be incidental. Above all, you must not mix your sense of self-worth or pride with your child's learning. Given time and a low-stress environment, your child will learn to understand and feel comfortable with numbers.

One last point—when your child brings home a worksheet, analyze it for the goal of the lesson, not just the number right or wrong. Work toward the goal through your game activities and through daily life. Don't teach the fact—teach the goal. Most of the previous activities were goal directed rather than specific fact oriented.

SECOND GRADE

In second grade, the child is expected to perform many of the same types of functions as in the first grade; however, there will be a greater spread in the number system. For example, in the second grade, the child is taught to master numeral order to 999. Number combinations that total between ten and twenty are learned. The concepts of weight and liquid measure frequently appear in this grade, and children learn terminology of shapes: triangle, square, circle, etc.

Late in the school year, the child should deal with regrouping. You probably called it borrowing when you were subtracting. However, regrouping is also a term used now in addition. Second graders learn such miscellaneous items as symbols for greater than and less than, thermometer reading, or making change. A readiness for multiplication is taught and assessed.

The authors have saved for last an item which research has shown to be a common failing of school children—the word problem. On national tests, this area is most frequently the area of greatest difficulty for students. A word problem is nothing more than that: a problem expressed in words. The difficult thing for children is to separate the essential elements from all the surrounding distractors. The best way to help your child is to use daily opportunities to express in words the mathematical situations that arise. For example, ask your child how many boys are in the class and how many girls. Say: "If there are thirteen boys and sixteen girls in the class, how many children are there in all?" You may then construct a problem by writing out the numerals. Alert your child to the fact that certain key words or phrases tell us whether to add or subtract. "In all" is such a phrase. Later on in second grade you can try: "How many more girls are there than boys?" The "more than" is a clue to subtract.

BACK TO BASICS

PARENTAL HELP

Place Value

Place value is a critical concept in the regrouping activity in the second grade. This is probably one area in which you will need to do direct teaching. One approach to teaching place value involves the odometer in your car. This device is especially useful in the tens and ones column. For example, show your child the progression of numerals on the tenths-of-a-mile wheel of your odometer. Have the child call out the numeral as you progress down the street. As the numeral eight approaches, alert the child to watch what happens in the column to the left. Caution—don't both of you watch so intently that an accident results!

Moving from car to kitchen, you can prepare a series of three yogurt cups for place value activity. Label the first cup with the ones label, the next one with the tens label, and the last one with the hundreds label. Use a nail that you have heated on the range top to punch nine randomly spaced holes in the lid of each yogurt cup. Provide your child with ten nails, each one shorter than the height of the yogurt cup. Say, "I'd like you to place these nails in the holes for me, and let's count them as you do so." As the child pushes each nail into a hole, you count: one, two, three, etc. As the ninth nail is inserted and all the holes are filled, you may ask, "What can we do with this nail?" If the child says, "We can put it in the next cup," you respond, "Right. That shows we have one ten. Now let's remove the nine nails from the ones cup and put them inside the tens cup." Lift the lid and drop the nine nails inside. It is important that your child realized that the one nail in the tens cup lid represents a group of ten nails (the nine inside and the one in the lid). If this activity continues to interest your child repeat it one more time so that you put another group of nine nails into the ones cup and one more in the tens cup. It is somewhat essential that your child be able to verbalize that the two nails in the tens cup are called "twenty," and that the two nails represent twenty single nails.

The operation of regrouping rests on the basis of the above concept. If the child can understand that we really don't "borrow" anything (to borrow implies that we will pay back), but that we regroup from the tens cup to the ones cup, he or she can see why it is possible to subtract a larger numeral from a smaller one when there is a numeral in the tens place. Too often, the concept of regrouping is taught in an abstract way without a true sense of the reality of the symbols we use in the ones, tens, and subsequent columns.

Greater and Less

In the second grade, children are taught the greater than symbol (>) and the less than symbol (<). These symbols along with the plus and minus signs are probably the first steps in developing symbol notation.

An easy way to communicate these two abstract symbols is to suggest to your child that these symbols remind you of an alligator with jaws open. The imagery is that the hungry alligator always wants to eat the larger item. So if your child sees $6 > 5$, he or she would read it, "Six is greater than five," or, $5 < 6$, would be read, "Five is less than six." The main assistance you are giving your child here is the alligator—an effective mnemonic device.

Shapes and Terms

The idea of naming shapes to identify them is generally concentrated on more heavily here than in the first grade. This topic was introduced in the preschool chapter, but it is now receiving formal attention in school. When you notice an object that is square, you might remark, "Please bring me that square-shaped Tupperware lid," or "Would you give me that rectangular block, please?" "No, not that one." "Yes, that's it." "Notice how it is more long than wide?" Through the use of such terminology in daily life, the child comes to associate the words with the reality.

Money, Time, and Distance

The topic of money is reintroduced in the second grade. Chances are that if you worked with your child with money earlier, readiness for more terms and denominations has been established.

In the first grade, it was suggested that you convert pennies into larger denominations of money. This continues to be useful in the second grade; however, you might convert smaller units into larger ones. For example, you might start giving your child a nickel a day for an allowance. This nickel could be converted into dimes at the end of six days, the dimes to quarters at regular intervals, and so on.

A chart for your child's room would help to show equivalencies. Use actual coins or photographs to show that five pennies equal one nickel, two nickels equal one dime, two dimes and one nickel equal one quarter, etc.

The concept of time is often a traumatic learning experience in school if it has not been introduced early, and in a matter-of-fact way at home. Don't make a big issue of telling time but do make a big issue of *using* the telling of time. For example, if there is a favorite television program, say to your child, "Sesame Street starts at nine o'clock. I'll set the hands of this clock at nine o'clock, and I'll put it here beside the electric clock. Watch the electric clock; and when it is the same as this one, you can turn on the TV."

Try to avoid the use of digital clocks when your child is learning to tell time. Digital clocks are a convenience, but they are a lazy way to know the time!

When possible, use first the hour and then the quarter hour for telling time. Go to dinner at 6:00 P.M., to the movie at 7:00 P.M., but always communicate to your child a statement of time and have him or her look at the clock. Use the: "Let's see what time it is!" statement to make your child conscious of the upcoming event and its time frame. Do not hesitate to give your child an old clock

98

whose hands he or she can manipulate. Use a paper pie plate marked into a clock face to let your child tell you when a favorite program comes on television.

In conclusion, use time as much as possible in your child's presence. State out loud that you are setting the oven timer for fifteen minutes so you can perform some special operation to an item cooking in the oven. Say, "Five, ten, fifteen," as you move the large hand to set the time.

Distance is another area introduced in the first grade and developed in the second grade. These repeated contacts with certain topics throughout the grades is referred to as the "spiral curriculum," meaning that a topic is encountered in one grade only to be reintroduced in a subsequent grade. This has advantages in the light of our mobile population and the child's developmental stages.

In assisting your child in distance measurement, a tape measure should be provided the first- or second-grade child. First of all, it is fun to snap it in and out. Secondly, most of them have a convenient angle on the end to attach to an item. Thirdly, the wise parent can find numerous items that "need" to be measured. "Johnny/Susie, please bring your tape measure to the kitchen. I need to measure this drawer, because I want to buy a new tray for the silverware. Let's go to the store and see how big those plastic trays are." Or, "How wide is this bathroom? We need to buy a new bath rug."

SUMMARY

It cannot be emphasized too strongly that you have the power and ability to educate your child indirectly if you will only do so. Children are great imitators. As you do a job, verbalize your thoughts as they relate to arithmetic in daily life. Say the hours, distances, fractions. Let your child encounter these in context, so that when the teacher introduces the symbol, word, or process, your child has a readiness based upon your closeness and the communications you have made.

BACK TO BASICS

THIRD GRADE

All of the preceding topics are covered in the third grade. Multiplication and division are added.

If you have been diligent in your communications with your child or children, if you have shown enthusiasm for mathematics yourself, there is a good chance your child will accept and enjoy mathematics.

PARENTAL HELP

You must fully understand the basic ideas of multiplying and dividing in order to help your child with these operations. Multiplication is a very high order of abstraction for the child who must be helped to understand that it is merely repeated addition. It is here that your earlier use of the word "sets" will assist you. One way of assisting your child to gain an operational understanding of multiplication is to dig out the building blocks in the toy box. Find six or eight blocks of the same size and shape. Arrange the blocks in sets of twos and in as many rows as you can:

Ask your child to add the blocks. Possibly he or she will count by twos: two, four, six, eight. Say, "Four sets of two each equals eight"; or (here you write the equation) four times two equals eight: $4 \times 2 = 8$. This process is almost identical to what the classroom teacher will do in introducing multiplication. Yet, if you do it in as informal a manner as possible it will be more likely to be received by your child as nonthreatening and nonteaching. It is extremely important that the child see and understand the concept behind the multiplication process. It is also important that the child know that the inverse is true: two times four equals eight.

Although much of the current teaching shies away from requiring memorizing the multiplication tables, it is highly valuable to memorize them for speed in computation. Therefore, it would be well for you to prepare a set of tables and do fun drills with your child. Try the "If you can say the two tables without a mistake, you may choose where we go for dinner" routine. "If you can say the three tables in thirty seconds, we'll stop and get an ice-cream cone," etc.

The use of word problems continues to play an important role in the mathematics education of your child. As you are going to the grocery store, try a few problems such as: "There are three rows of canned goods at this store. Each of them has six shelves. How many shelves are there?" If your child has the correct answer (eighteen), say, "Tell how you got that answer. What did you do?" It is important to help the child verbalize the process in multiplication, because it reinforces understanding. Before you pounce requesting that the information be verbalized, be sure that you have expressed pleasure or at least approval that your child has answered correctly! Reinforcement is your best ally.

Remember, it is not the purpose of this chapter to make you an arithmetic teacher. Rather it is to sensitize you to the basic concepts needed to reinforce your child's learning. Continue to look for opportunities to do multiplication in word problems. Use the postal boxes in the post office. You might ask, "How many boxes are there on this wall? Count the rows and the boxes in one row. What would you do to find the total number of boxes?"

Division is the inverse or undoing of multiplication. Again, use your set of eight blocks. Mix the blocks so that they are not in a pattern. Ask, "How many sets of two blocks can you make from these eight blocks?" As the child orders the blocks in sets of two, say, "Eight divided by two equals four." Then, "How many sets of four can you make?" When this is accomplished, say, "Eight divided by four equals two." Refer to the earlier episode when you helped your child discover that four times two equals eight.

Assisting your child in multiplication and division is complex and time consuming. The process should evolve slowly and sequentially and should be done with considerable patience and with many illustrations and manipulative materials.

SUMMARY

In summary, it is best to avoid much direct teaching. Instead, seek to reinforce your child's conceptual understanding by bringing the operations of multiplication and division into many daily activities.

PART FOUR

Moving Ahead: The Upper Grades

CHAPTER **8** **Reading**

The child's home environment is still a major factor in reading achievement of children in the upper grades.

ONCE YOUR CHILD was able to read in the primary grades and the report card indicated to you that she or he was succeeding in this area, you probably thought that your work was through and that you could rest from this most important task. This is not true. Your child in the upper elementary grades still needs your help. In fact, your help is probably more needed at this point than ever, because reading skills are essential to learning the various subjects in school courses. Remember the slogan: "In the primary grades we learn to read and in the upper grades we read to learn." There are four vital areas of reading in which you can help your child be a success in school during these grades: motivation, vocabulary, comprehension, and study skills.

MOTIVATION

Motivation is essential to keep your child reading. The child must continue to practice the skills of reading over and over again so that these skills will be strengthened and will continue to grow.

BACK TO BASICS

Motivation gives an incentive to action in reading that will keep your child reading the materials that must be learned to succeed in school work. To provide inspiration for your child in reading, you can develop his or her interest, you can allow your child to share what is being read, and you can help him or her appreciate what is being read.

Interest

Children's attitudes toward reading are greatly reflected in their parents' attitudes toward reading. If the child perceives that the parent has little interest or concern about the subject to be read, the child will not approach the assignment with enthusiasm. Here are some ways that the parents can help:

1. Be enthusiastic about reading the subject being studied by your child. Discuss it and add some practical knowledge you have to the discussion.
2. Provide him or her with appropriate instructional materials, such as a dictionary, an encyclopedia and, of course paper and pencil.
3. Help your child to establish the purpose for the reading assignment. Ask, "What answers must you find in this selection?" Purpose helps to direct your child toward being an active reader looking for some verbal or written response to the selection read.

Jonathan only likes to read dog stories. His mother suggested that he read *Call of the Wild*. Not only did this book meet his need to read about dogs, but it also led Jonathan into the rough northern gold-mining country, to discover the differences among human beings, to the world of the animal kingdom other than dogs, and to understand how people learn to cope with problems. Parents can influence their child to discover new vistas of learning, to extend his or her curiosity into other areas, and to expand his or her current fascination in a particular area. By this extension of interest, the child may discover new horizons and thus be motivated to continue to read other books and materials when the interest in dogs begins to wane.

Sharing

Unmotivated children can become reluctant readers. These reluctant readers are those children who can read, but who would rather not read. Eventually, these children will fall behind in reading compared to their classmates. Many reports have shown that the parents are the best source for motivating children to become active readers. The major responsibility for help in this area lies with the parents for the development of attitudes and habits so that the child will be an active reader rather than a reluctant reader.

The development of a favorable attitude toward reading obviously involves the availability of books. Your child must have books available to read. The school library or public library can supplement your child's home library.

The best time to promote interest and good attitudes about reading occurs when your child has read an interesting book and wants to share it with you. There are many and varied ways that your child could share the book just read. One way is to have your child just retell the story. This is a very simple approach, yet it increases your child's involvement with the book.

Marc read every free moment he had, not only in class, but at home as well. His mother, who was the school secretary, caught him many times in bed with the covers over his head with a flashlight reading a book. All of a sudden his teacher noticed that he was not handing in book reports. When his teacher asked why he wasn't handing in book reports Marc replied, "I'm not reading any books." The teacher said, "Marc, you liked to read earlier this year. I can't understand why you are not reading now!" "Well, the truth is," replied Marc, "I can't stand writing the book reports that are required in this class!" The very task of book reporting that was to spur children on to read was defeating the whole free reading program for Marc. There is not just one way to share a book. Even in school where book reports are required there are many viable ways of sharing books.

These are some other appropriate ways to share books:

1. Read a part from the book that he or she really likes.
2. Using a tape recorder or cassette recorder, make an announcement advertising the book as one does on television or radio.
3. Describe a humorous incident from the book.
4. Dramatize some aspect of the book.
5. Project oneself into the role of a favorite book character and act out that role.
6. Complete a project from a how-to-do-it book.

You can develop interest by reading to your child from books which would be too difficult for the child to read. This type of sharing develops an attitude that reading is important as you subtly show enthusiastic interest in your own reading, as well as stretching the interest of your child in listening to more difficult reading.

Appreciation

To sustain motivation for reading in the upper elementary grades, your child must develop an appreciation for reading different materials. You, as a parent, can help by assisting in three important appreciation skills: visualization, responsiveness, and creativity.

In reading short stories, novels, or other reading materials, visualization skills are essential for the child to truly enjoy reading. The child's ability to visualize the action, the setting, and the roles played by the characters is an important skill to help the child enjoy what he or she is reading. As a parent, you can help him or her learn to visualize by discussing with your child the parts of the reading materials that could clearly give a visual picture. Ask questions concerning what is going on in the story, where the action is taking place, and how the child would feel if he or she were a particular character in the story. Asking these types of questions will help your child conjure in his or her mind the unfolding drama of the story content. *This visualization skill is what makes reading more exciting than watching television.*

Once this skill is developed, one can create much more exciting events than can be shown on television because of the limitation of the television media compared to the mind of an active reader.

In developing responsiveness skills within your child, it is important to point out to your child that reading is the receptive end of writing. The author is writing to the reader about a certain event, activity, or such and is trying to convey his or her feelings, attitudes, and information. The reader needs to realize that he or she can also respond to the author, not person-to-person or in any direct communicative manner, but in his or her mind by agreeing or disagreeing with the author or the materials presented. The response could be pleasure from reading what the author has to say or not wanting to read anything written by the author again. Responding in this manner makes the reader more involved in the reading process and should motivate him or her to further reading because one is actively involved. To develop this skill within your child, again you must take the time to discuss the author's ideas and help him or her to respond actively to the materials written. Through questions, you can help your child make valid responses and direct his or her feelings about the material read.

Creativity is the third element in developing appreciation, which in turn motivates the reader. A creative reader is one who can "read between the lines." Reading between the lines of print means that the reader is able to infer what the author means when he or she doesn't exactly write down everything that could be reported. The author wrote, "Janelle said, 'Go jump in the lake,' and at that moment, Jeanne quickly left and went directly to her bedroom." Now did the author really mean that Janelle wanted Jeanne to jump in the lake? No, this was an expression of disgust. Your child will need to know and understand that an author does not necessarily write down exactly everything that he or she may want the reader to understand. You will need to help your child derive meaning from what is written by determining what the author really means. The best approach to this is to help your child read tall-tale stories and then derive meaning from these stories by discussing what the author was really trying to get over to the reader. After your child understands how to interpret tall-tale stories, you can work into other fictional materials and finally into factual reading materials.

VOCABULARY

Vocabulary development is as important as motivation in helping your child in reading in the upper grades. The need to improve one's vocabulary never ceases. In the upper grades, the vocabulary becomes more varied and difficult compared to the word work in the lower elementary grades. As a parent, you can help your child in vocabulary development by teaching him or her how to use synonyms, contextual clues, and the dictionary and even to develop his or her own personal dictionary.

Synonyms

In using synonyms for vocabulary development, you will need to remember that these words have highly *similar* meanings; in the English language it is rare to find words that have exact meanings. To help your child in developing his or her vocabulary by the use of synonyms, point out sentence structures that assist your child in achieving meaning. The word may be defined within the sentence, such as "To forsake is to abandon the individual." *Forsake* is defined by the synonym *abandon,* thus the child can understand the meaning by the use of a synonym for the word *forsake.* If these clues are not available, you can help your child, as he or she is reading, by supplying a synonym for an unknown word which will aid in the understanding of that word. Understanding synonyms will help your child develop vocabulary understanding as well as comprehension skills. It is not enough to be able to pronounce the word; your child must be able to understand its meaning.

Contextual Clues

Since the meaning of words depends upon their placement in context, vocabulary words are best learned from the printed page rather than in isolation. Your child can learn the meaning of unknown words by using the words within the sentence or phrase to clarify the meaning of the unknown word. You will need to point out ways that this is done. Sometimes the unknown word is defined within the statement, such as *"Dexterity* means skill and ease in using the hands." Another example of an author using contextual clues to assist the reader through definition is: "Her *dexterity* in playing the piano demonstrated skill and ease in using her hands." As a parent, you can tell your child to continue to read the sentence skipping the unknown word. Then have your child go back to the unknown word and determine if he or she can give the definition for it. Many times, your child will be able to understand the word merely by reading the other words in the sentence.

Dictionary

If all else fails in your child's attempts to understand the vocabulary words in the reading materials, then the dictionary is available to give the outside help needed to assist your child in reading. It is important that you teach your child how to use the dictionary and encourage him or her to use it whenever necessary. Many young people know how to use the dictionary but fail to utilize this most important skill because of the time it takes to look up the word; thus, your encouragement is absolutely necessary.

The first thing you as a parent need to do in this area is select the proper dictionary. The dictionary you select must not be too difficult. Often parents make the mistake of getting a dictionary that is beyond the reading level of the child. The definitions in these dictionaries sometimes contain words unknown to the child, which makes the dictionary difficult for the child to use properly. Get a simple, easy dictionary and, when your child grows out of it because his or her reading level increases, you can always get another one.

The parent needs to survey the dictionary to determine what it has to offer. The parent may need to practice using the pronunciation guide of the dictionary with the child and familiarize him or her with any special features of the dictionary purchased.

Your child must be brought to realize that although each entry word in the dictionary is only one word, the definition is usually more than one word; therefore, he or she must be able to derive meaning as that word is used in a phrase or sentence. The meaning must be "turned back" into the phrase or sentence to determine if it is the one desired. For example, the word *run* has over eighty different definitions listed in some dictionaries; and yet this is a rather easy word to pronounce. Turning the word *run* back into the phrase or sentence is necessary in order to know which one of the definitions is correct. For example, "John plans to *run* to the bank, because there is a *run* on withdrawals and he needs the money to *run* for election." It is necessary to look up the word *run* in the dictionary and then find the corrrect definition for each *run* in the sentence. The process of taking the definition that fits and applying it to the sentence is called "turning back." Thus after the definitions are turned back into the sentence, the sentence would read: "John plans to *go at a pace faster than a walk* to the bank, because there is a *persistent heavy demand* on withdrawals, and he needs the money to *contend in a race* for election." Many times, children cannot understand which definition to use, because they have not been taught how to "turn back" the definitions into the sentence to see if it does indeed make sense.

There are several ways one can learn to turn back into context the definitions from a dictionary. This can be done by substitution, transposition, and paraphrasing.

Substitution: He was considered *brilliant* by his peers.
He was considered *very intelligent* by his peers.
Transposition: The immigration officers would not *admit* him into the United States.
The immigration officers would not *allow* him *to enter* the United States.
Paraphrasing: The rich man has many *obedient* servants.
The rich man has servants *who are doing what they are told to do.*

In helping your child use the dictionary properly, it is important that you provide many easy and simple examples until he or she understands how one can turn the definition back into the phrase or sentence being read for understanding.

Personal Dictionary

In addition to purchasing a dictionary, it would be very helpful for your child to keep a personal dictionary made of the words that he or she has had difficulty in defining or pronouncing. You need only to get a binder with empty pages. Have your child place a letter of the alphabet on top of each page. As your child meets a word that causes him or her a problem, he or she should look it up in the purchased dictionary and then write down the word plus a simple definition and the pronouncing guide for that word. If a looseleaf binder is used, pages can be added so that alphabetical sequence will not be destroyed as the original pages are filled with words.

One advantage of a personal dictionary is that the mere act of writing the unknown word, definition, and pronouncing guide will reinforce the use of the word in your child's mind. Also your child will have a list of words to review and check against as the need arises rather than looking up the word in a commercial dictionary. Another advantage of the personal dictionary is that it can act as concrete evidence to show that he or she has mastered these words and should bring a great deal of satisfaction to your child.

COMPREHENSION

Vocabulary development is essential to comprehension. As your child uses the skills learned in vocabulary development, he or she will be able to understand more fully the written materials which are necessary for success in school. As a parent, you can assist your child in improving comprehension skills in the reading process. The techniques for this goal include previewing, underlining, graphic responses, and the cloze procedure.

Previewing

Previewing, which is sometimes referred to as surveying, is an organized preliminary look at the reading material to be read. This could be the reading assignment given to your child, a section, a chapter, or the entire book. Previewing is most useful for your child when he or she is reading expository materials, but can be done for other types of reading also.

The use of the following steps by your child, with your help if necessary, will teach him or her the technique of previewing:

1. Have the child read the title, the introduction, the summary (if the materials assigned to be read has one), and the side headings and glance at each picture, graph, or chart.
2. If questions are posed by the author, have the child read each question carefully.
3. Have the child recall what is already known about the topic to be read.
4. Have the child predict what kinds of information he or she expects the article to offer or what questions he or she expects it to answer.
5. Have the child develop questions from the material previewed. At first, these questions should be written down. After the skill is mastered, these questions could be kept in the child's head. To begin with, questions could be formulated by changing the side headings into questions. For example, a side heading which reads, "Causes of an Economic Depression" could be changed into a question, "What are the causes of an economic depression?"

The whole purpose of previewing is to get your child ready to read the materials assigned so that he or she will be able to understand what is being read. This previewing gives your child the proper mind-set by familiarizing him or her with the material to read and sets goals for your child by having questions to answer, thus helping your child be an active, aggressive reader.

Underlining

Underlining is another technique that can help your child to understand better what he or she is reading. Research has indicated that utilizing an underlining technique improves reading comprehension and helps the reader to remember important items. If the book belongs to the child or if it is possible to underline important words, phrases, or main ideas, this technique can be very helpful. However, if the book in which the assignments have been made cannot be written in, the items that you would normally underline would have to be written out on a separate piece of paper. Whether underlining or note making, the skill remains essentially the same.

When teaching your child to underline, you should point out to your child to underline key words and phrases in such a way that when the underlined words are read together, they will make sense in a normal, smooth flow of words. A second way to use this technique is to underline the main ideas found in the reading materials. In English writing, the main idea is most generally found in the first or last sentence of a paragraph. Research has also indicated that underlining done by your child will give better results than if the underlining is done by you. However, underlining done by you for your child will increase comprehension and recall.

Graphic Responses

Another approach to improving comprehension of reading materials is through the graphic-response technique. Not all responses to show understanding need to be written or orally discussed. Many children can remember longer and understand better if the material read can be responded to by some form of graphics. For instance, a pie chart is the easiest way to understand the concept of a school budget. Another useful graphic is a time line illustrating what happens sequentially in a story. This helps your child understand the relationship that time has to the events of the story.

A third approach to graphic responses for improving comprehension is a mapping technique. After reading the materials assigned, your child can map out the relationships that exist in the story content. The following is an example of mapping an article read on Alaska:

115

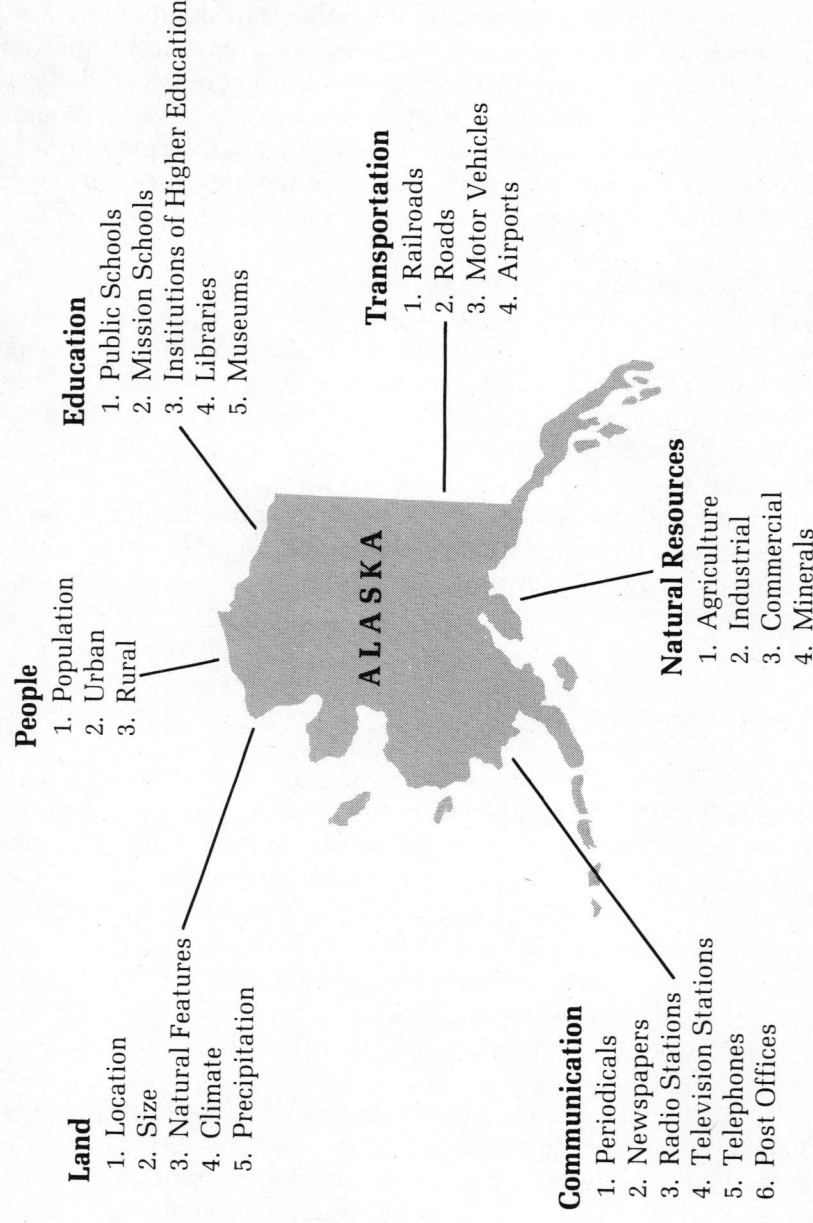

Education
1. Public Schools
2. Mission Schools
3. Institutions of Higher Education
4. Libraries
5. Museums

Transportation
1. Railroads
2. Roads
3. Motor Vehicles
4. Airports

People
1. Population
2. Urban
3. Rural

Natural Resources
1. Agriculture
2. Industrial
3. Commercial
4. Minerals

ALASKA

Land
1. Location
2. Size
3. Natural Features
4. Climate
5. Precipitation

Communication
1. Periodicals
2. Newspapers
3. Radio Stations
4. Television Stations
5. Telephones
6. Post Offices

116

The purpose for graphic response is that it helps your child to see pictorially the major concepts being read. Some children can do better using graphics to aid understanding than answering questions found in the reading materials. Some reading material lends itself better to graphic responses than other responses for comprehension improvement.

Cloze Procedure

The cloze procedure is yet another way to aid your child in understanding what he or she reads. The cloze procedure allows your child to interact with the writer of the materials being read. This is an excellent procedure for developing understanding and comprehension.

The first step of the cloze procedure is to go through the reading material that has been assigned and block out every tenth word with sticky tape. Another approach is to use a clear piece of plastic placed over the page and blacken every tenth word with a crayon. Then have your child read the material silently and go back and put in the word or a synonym for the word in each blank space. This procedure heightens your child's awareness of the words as they relate to understanding the material read. Your child is required to interact with the author each tenth word, thus increasing his or her comprehension skills.

STUDY SKILLS

After you have helped to motivate your child in wanting to read and you have worked with him or her in improving vocabulary and comprehension skills, you will need to help him or her in the study skills needed to keep on learning. The study skills that you can help your child acquire are how to survey textbooks, how to strengthen memory, and how to develop library skills.

117

Survey of Textbooks

An excellent study skill technique that you can teach your child is how to survey his or her textbooks. Before reading is started, each child should survey the textbooks that will be used for classroom work. Under your guidance, your child can learn how to use this skill to further his or her understanding of the textbook and how to use the format of the textbook to aid learning.

Point out to your child the parts of a textbook such as the table of contents, title page, glossary, and index. This knowledge of textbook parts will help your child learn how to use the textbook format quickly to find out where in the textbook the answers can be found. The table of contents outlines the major topics that will be treated in the textbook. The title page gives information concerning not only the title of the book but something about the author. The glossary is like a small dictionary used for ease of pronouncing and defining the textbook words. The index gives your child a quick way to find facts and other details from the book.

This type of information will help your child realize the purpose and value of these textbook aids to learning. Reading requires a great deal of finding materials and organizing them for learning. This knowledge of textbook parts will assist your child in finding specific materials quickly.

Memory Aids

You have probably found yourself reading and learning a certain topic, and yet when you tried to recall this valuable information at a later date, you could not remember the material well enough to use what you had studied previously. This is a common problem many of us, including your child, have in recalling information. You can assist your child in developing some aids or techniques that will assist him or her in remembering. To improve memory, the major task for the reader is to get the information in some type of a personal, logically structured format.

What might be a logically structured format for one may not be for others—that is why it must be personalized. Even when items given by the teacher in school are logically structured by the teacher, many children fail to remember the information, because they do not fit the child's personal structure.

You can teach your child the use of rhymes or rhythm to help him or her in memory. Remember this example: "Thirty days hath September, April, June, and November; all the rest have thirty-one except February, which usually has twenty-eight"? The rhythm and rhyme of this saying is what helps you remember the number of days in each month.

Another approach to aid memory is to help your child associate what he or she needs to remember with something else that is familiar. A typical example is remembering how to use the proper spelling for *principal* by associating that he or she is your "pal," not your "ple." This memory technique helps your child to remember through association.

A third approach to help in remembering is through the use of acronyms. Acronyms are formed by using the first letters of words to remember, such as *HOMES*, to help in remembering the Great Lakes: *H* for Lake Huron, *O* for Lake Ontario, *M* for Lake Michigan, *E* for Lake Erie, and *S* for Lake Superior. The use of acronyms for various governmental agencies is a quite common aid in remembering the proper flow of words, for instance *NASA* for National Aeronautics and Space Administration.

Your child may be able to remember better if what he or she must remember is pictured in some way. A crude drawing of a model, flow chart, or a picture may help your child to remember what is required. The concreteness of the pictorial representation may be exactly what is needed to help your child remember the process or the connection of the material to be remembered.

Library Skills

In many schools, your child may have been taught very well to use the library; however, you must not leave this to chance. You should take your child to the public library and ask pertinent questions of your child to see if in fact he or she does know how to use the library in an efficient manner. If you do not know all the details of the library, you too can ask the librarian, and the two of you can get an orientation for the use of the library.

Your child should be aware of these particular areas of the library:

1. Use of the card catalog (including the use of the three types of bibliographic cards: subject, author, and title cards).
2. Use of the Dewey Decimal System and Library of Congress System.
3. Use of the periodical index.
4. Use of circulation and reference materials.
5. Use of special collections.

Often a child who has abilities to do well in schoolwork has difficulty doing well in library research because he or she lacks the skills needed to effectively use the library. It is important that your child has knowledge in locating and using the library to do research or other types of assignments given by the teachers to supplement work done in school. The library is a storehouse for learning but only if your child knows how to tap the many resources available.

SUMMARY

In the upper grades, your child still needs your influence to assist him or her in reading achievement. Through your help and your child's efforts, success can be achieved in school. Motivation is a key to this success. If your child is sufficiently motivated, he or she will continue to read, thus practicing this most important skill. Growth in reading takes place only through reading, through practicing reading, and then reading some more.

Don't get discouraged as you are working with your child in reading. All of these suggestions cannot be taught at once, but must be spaced over a period of time. Your time available to your child for this assistance is limited, so use your time to work in the areas most needed at the present time. Helping your child succeed in school is important. Remember how important this success is in each of our lives for our own personal development. Keep working with your child so both of you can be happier and more successful in the business of learning.

CHAPTER 9 Writing

"How do I know what I think until I see what I say?"

(Attributed to E. M. Forster)

CHILDREN IN THE upper elementary grades should be free to experiment with language in their writing. Most often such experimentation will occur in their story-type writing. Although the main thrust of this chapter will be towards facilitating the writing of more "expository"-type compositions, it is important to know about, appreciate, and encourage the creativity expressed in such compositions. Let's consider three compositions characteristic of upper elementary children who have been encouraged to write.

The following story illustrates how a sensitivity to language, developed through reading and writing, intersects with a fourth grader's fascination with microcomputers:

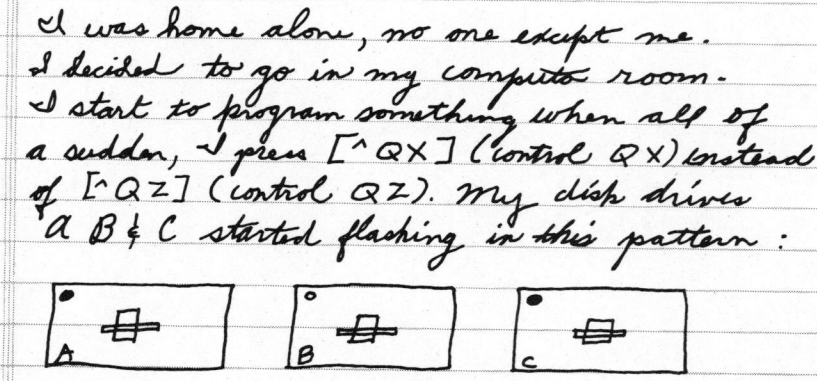

I was home alone, no one except me. I decided to go in my computer room. I start to program something when all of a sudden, I press [^QX] (control QX) instead of [^QZ] (control QZ). My disk drives A B & C started flashing in this pattern:

And I knew they weren't supposed to.
And then, I felt a sudden jerk and then
a little dim light, and then it grew
brighter, brighter, did it stop? No, wait a
minute, and then the light was almost
blinding.

   And then lights were all around me.
Then I saw this in front of me:
          ᴎOᴙT-Ǝ⅃I⅂
   ᴙᴙTX.8ᑫᑫ .oᴎ YTIᴙUƆƎƧ
"Dang!" I said. "I'm trapped in my
own good use of file!" Then I saw
an arrow comming toward me.

   "Cursor!" I exclaimed. (Cursor is
the figure that moves the ▓ to different
parts of the screen.) Then, when it
came past me, I grabbed hold of it
"This is like riding on the back of an
M X missle," I thought.

   Then I heard a noise. It sounded
like someone was calling me. And
then, the next thing I know, I was
sitting up in my bed with my mother
saying "Come on. It is 10 o'clock in
the morning! Oh, by the way, you left
your computer on last night."

Imagination is exercised here, of course. Note also, however, the writer's awareness of the reader by acknowledging the possibility that the reader may not know what a "cursor" is.

The following piece, "Chapter One," was written by a fourth grader killing time at the typewriter in his father's office late one afternoon. Like some of the sample compositions in Chapter 6, this piece may illustrate a "therapeutic" purpose, or perhaps simply a relief at no longer experiencing the unpleasant feelings described.

```
                    CHAPTER ONE


             Today was the day.  The first day of school at my new school.
      I had moved all the way across the country in a car from Georgia to
      Nevada.  I knew I was going to make some new friends (or at least I
      thought I was going to make some new friends!)  today.  I just had eaten
      breakfast and was ready to walk to school.  When I got to school, I wanted
      to make some new friends.  When I had gotten up this morning I had
      said I was going to make some new friends.  Well, boy was I wrong!
      The day went by very slowly because there was no one to play with and hardly
      any word.  When I got home, I told my mom all about my first day at school
      and she said " I'm sure that you will make some new friends tomorrow or
      the next day." Ba humbug!  In fact it took me quite a few weeks untill I
      met anyone.My first friend's name was Gavin.  He was such a nice and friendly
      person.
```

So ended the chronicle of this lad's move to a new home. This beginning to a "book" never got farther than this one paragraph! Nevertheless, the writing served its purpose. Children will need assistance in school in developing their many ideas, but we should not despair at so many compositions started and then abandoned. In this respect, young writers are similar to just about every great writer who ever lived!

This next composition, although a bit lengthy, is included to illustrate the modeling of a particular genre—the detective story— and an increasing sophistication of language forms and vocabulary. These latter aspects are a bit awkward, but they are the forerunners of more mature writing:

THE MYSTERY OF MR. GUNMAN'S DEATH

One day, Jimmy Gordon was sitting on the front porch steps with his sister, Katie Gordon. "I'm bord," said Jimmy. "Me too!" said Katie. "Nothing exiting happens around here any more." Jimmy agreed. "That is unless your counting the time when Mrs. Waterman had the minnows coming out of the kitchen faucet!" Jimmy said. "No" said Katie "I mean like a safe cracking or something." Jimmy said "We haven't had one of those since 1924! And I don't think we"ll have one of those for a long time. Because the guy, I think his name was Johnathan Henry or something like that, served a 20 year sentence in prison!"

"Well, I still think there's going to be some kind of a crime around here soon, I can feel it in my bones," said Katie.

"Don't get your hopes up," said Jimmy. "And besides, Christmas is coming so we'll have something to play with," Jimmy said.

Just at that moment their mom came out. "Jimmy and Katie, it's almost dinner time."

Jimmy and Kate both said together "Oh, mom." Jimmy said "By the way, what is for dinner ?" His mom answered "We're having pizza...."Goodie!" Jimmy and Katie interupted.

"Wait, let me finish" said their mom "Your father and I are having pizza, and you're having liver." "Yuck!" said Jimmy and Katie. "Can't we skip dinner tonight ?" said Jimmy.

"No, but I suppose you could have a couple of pieces of pizza," said there mom. Jimmy and Katie looked relieved. And right at that point they heard a cry of pain from next door, Mr. Gunman's house. Jimmy and Katie rused over to help him. "Wait!" cried their mom "Come back it might be dangerous!"

"Danger's my middle name!" said Jimmy. They heard the cries get softer and softer but they were getting closer and closer. They they heard a soft "Help!" and looked down. And they saw Mr. Gunman laying on the floor. Jimmy asked "What happened ?" Mr.

BACK TO BASICS

Gunman said nothing except "Find the cause of my death," and then he fell silent. "Jimmy! Call the parimedics!"said Katie.

Jimmy said calmly, "It's too late." "I wish we could do something Kat." Katie said, "I guess we better go home and call the police."

"Yeh, I guess so." When they got home, they told of the catastrophy.

"That sounds horrible!" exclaimed their mom. When the police got there, they asked if they knew how their neighbor died. Katie said "We really don't know. All he said was Find the cause of my death." That night Jimmy sat threre in his bed thinking about the coincident. Jimmy shouted,"I got it!"He went to wake Katie.

"You got what?" asked Katie.

"A safe cracking!"shouted Jimmy "Mr. Gunman has a safe, right? So, someone had to have murdered him in order to crack the safe at that time. The person who murdered Mr. Gunman thought that people would figure that since he was so old, that he would have a heart attack or something."

"Yeh, that makes since. But how did you know they were after the safe?"

"Oh no! I forgot to tell the police that I got a glipse of the safe and I saw that it was cracked!" That morning they called the police. The police went to Johnathen Henry and ordered him to come to court this instant. In the courtroom, Mr. Henry confessed that he killed Mr. Gunman to get the money because he had just lost a job and needed more money for a new job and didn't want to do it, but he had a family to feed. The next day, was Mr. Gunman's funeral. Mr. Henry and his family went to it. Mr. Henry got put in the slammer for 20 years. Mrs. Henry got a job during Mr. Henry's sentence, and was paid well for it.

THE END

126

Another interesting point about this story: It was co-authored. Two fifth graders collaborated at a word processor and inadvertently demonstrated what many researchers and educators have recently been emphasizing: the value of working with one or more peers in the process of writing.

THE WRITING PROCESS

Researchers who have studied the writing process have learned much from "real" writers—those who, like William Faulkner, Ernest Hemingway, Katherine Anne Porter, have produced acknowledgedly great works of literature. How did *they* write? Surprisingly, writing can be quite an *active* process. Actually, very few of the greats positioned themselves in a stiff-backed chair for assigned periods of time, unable to get up and chastised for deciding a particular piece of paper was not acceptable and tossing it into the wastebasket. They were in fact quite active, getting up and down, pacing back and forth, spending considerable periods of time gazing at the wall or out the window. Hemingway, for example, was said to write much of the time standing up. When your child is creating a first draft or engaged in "prewriting," do not insist on the "sit up straight, hold your pencil right" school of proper writing.

In Chapter 3 we mentioned the writing process and the steps by which young writers can get ready to write, prepare a first draft, revise, and proofread. In the upper elementary grades, the "revision" and "proofreading" stages become very important. Furthermore, the degree to which the first two steps are developed is greater. These students still may need help in understanding that what they write when they first put pen to paper does not have to be perfect or the "final copy." Revision and change is usually necessary and is quite natural.

Children at this level need to learn two things: (1) how to determine what they want to find out about and to write about, and (2) how to organize this knowledge for expression in writing. These areas should be the focus of their instruction in expository

127

writing in school, and you can play a most helpful role in this development at home.

"PERSONAL" REPORTS

As in so many areas that we have discussed in this book, *talking* with your child can be the foundation for helping him or her with expository writing. This holds true whether your child has been given an assignment to "write about something that you are interested in" or "write about the most important European explorers of the sixteenth century." In each case, it is necessary for your child to determine what he or she already knows about whatever is to be written. Talking brings this out, and good teachers will take advantage of this to get their students "brainstorming" about a topic—in the process, the teachers will write down words or phrases that the students come up with; these can be examined later for their relevance to the topic.

Prewriting

You may want to try this type of "brainstorming" with your child, or at least model the process once or twice so that your child will then be able to do this on his or her own. Let's follow through how you might help with this if your child was given the first type of assignment mentioned above, the "write about what you're interested in" topic. This sounds simple enough, but it is amazing how many children suddenly believe, *confronted with a blank sheet of paper,* that there is really nothing much that they *are* interested in! You can help by suggesting some of the areas that you know they have some interest in. This need not be a simple listing on your part; you can frame the statement with something like:

"You know, Jennifer, I've been impressed lately with how much you seem to know about computers. This could be something you would have a lot to share about with whoever would read your report."

By showing that you value what your daughter knows about a

particular area—and children really *do* know a lot—you are giving her a sense of the worth of her ideas and her knowledge. However, you may still have to help her brainstorm, as many children will still be hesitant to set about the task of writing.

Sitting with your child and having a pad of paper in hand, suggest, "Let's just think about some things that have to do with computers and how they may be of use to us." Your "brainstorm" list may look like the following:

Helps us with writing
Helps to do math
Helps us relax by playing games
Helps us to make designs and art

Jennifer decides that the report would be too long if she deals with all four of these topics, so she elects to write on the first two—writing and math. You can then suggest that she list ideas that occur to her that have to do with both writing and math. She will decide which of these ideas she will write about, and in which order. *Now* she is ready to write.

Writing

Jennifer's report discusses how easy it is to use the microcomputer for writing. She emphasizes the ease of making changes and the convenience of being able to put so much writing on one disk instead of having a lot of paper lying around. She goes on to discuss how the microcomputer helps families plan budgets and keep track of paying the bills—the points she decided to emphasize when she thought further about the microcomputer's role in computation.

Revising and Proofreading

After completing two pages in which she discusses to her satisfaction the points she wanted to make, Jennifer rereads her report. She decides that it is more important first to emphasize how microcomputers make it possible to store large amounts of writing than to discuss the ease of writing. She changes a couple of words in her discussion of the computational aspects. Satisfied with the writing, she then rereads the report to catch any misspellings and to check on proper punctuation. Now will come the time to copy the final product neatly for the final draft.

You can also facilitate these last two parts of the writing process. After reading your child's composition, feel free to ask a question or two. You can help your child determine whether he or she has clearly and appropriately conveyed what they intended to say. Importantly, children should learn that it is okay to have a messy paper at the stages prior to copying for the final draft!

REPORTS BASED UPON NEW INFORMATION

After your child gets a "feel" for writing a report drawing primarily upon his or her own experiences, the next step is to write a report based primarily on *new* information. Within the context of the writing process, children need help in the following:

1. framing their questions
2. obtaining information and formulating answers
3. structuring and writing final drafts

Moreover, the phase involving obtaining information is very challenging—children who are given no assistance here are those children whose final reports are often copied directly from the encyclopedia. Such reports do not reflect willful plagiarism; they are typical examples of honest, albeit untutored, attempts at report writing.

Prewriting

The first experience with writing a report based on new information involves obtaining information from a "live" source rather than from an inert book. Some children can handle the transition quite nicely; most should be encouraged to consult a first-hand source first. Following is an example of how "new" information can be obtained, organized, and written up in a report.

A popular and accessible source of information for children resides in their community—or even in their home. People's *occupations* are particularly fertile ground for investigation. Children can prepare for an interview with an adult in which questions are written ahead of time and the "interview" then taped on a cassette recorder. The interviewee's responses can then be paraphrased and written up. Important information concerning the interviewee's background will be included in the first paragraph, perhaps along with information about why the person came to be involved with that particular occupation. Possible additional questions are:

1. What kind of preparation (education, special training) is necessary for your occupation?
2. Have you always done this kind of work?
3. What do you like best about your work? What do you like least?
4. What is the most difficult part of your work?
5. What advice would you give to someone who is interested in doing what you do?
6. When you're not working, what do you like to do?
7. If you could do any type of work at all that you wanted, what would you do?

Writing, Revising, and Proofreading

The young writer has now to decide which questions and responses may be of most interest to the reader. These are then sequenced and the report written. Revising and proofreading occur just as they did in the "personal report" discussed above.

As we've suggested, the sequence in helping your child learn this type of writing places the role of books and reference materials and sources *later* in the learning process after the child has learned how to collect, analyze, and write up information. Your child is now familiar with an *active* approach to information seeking; he comes armed with questions and possibly speculations that will guide his search so that when he consults a particular book on the subject under investigation he will not attempt to read through every page and note every little detail. Rather, he is *selective* and looks for information relevant to his concerns.

Your child is now ready for the next type of report.

REPORT BASED ON BOOKS AND REFERENCE MATERIAL

Prewriting

Suppose your fifth grader is writing a report on how space might be used in the future. Through discussion about what is interesting and important about space, you have helped your child to narrow the focus to two areas: (1) space exploration and (2) using space for purposes of economic development. You may muse aloud at this point: "I wonder . . . Is it possible that space could be used to make things that people could use here on earth . . . What would it be like to be involved in that?"

Having gotten the "questioning" ball rolling, you can now consider this question with your child: If space is going to be used to manufacture all sorts of things for use here on earth, how will people live in space for long periods of time? As you talk this through, subsidiary questions arise, and at this point it is wise to jot these down as they occur to the two of you:

> Will the areas in which people live need to be fairly spacious, or will people adapt to living in small quarters for long periods of time?

> Will people get their food from earth or will they grow it in space?

> If the food is to be grown in space, what sorts of facilities/structures will be necessary?

> How *long* can people stay in space at any one time? Will it be necessary to return to earth fairly often?

Will "manufacturing" areas and "living" areas be kept apart or will they be in the same area?

Will an "earth"-type community develop? Will there be people living there whose jobs are not directly involved with manufacturing but with other areas, like running stores and shops?

These questions can lead to the consideration of space stations or colonies and, the more one ponders, to the possibility of creating entire *ecosystems* in space. By now the interest and excitement about the topic should help sustain the serious work of locating, organizing, and expressing information.

As your child looks for books in the library, the questions that have been raised will guide his or her selection. Titles of books can of course be good clues, but it may be necessary to review with the child how to scan the table of contents and the index to make sure that helpful information is contained within the text. Of course, once books are selected the child will not need to read *everything* in the book—a common assumption among many children! Rather, only the relevant portions of the text will be consulted.

Writing

Once the important information is located, it must be *paraphrased*. Learning to paraphrase is the first step toward eventually organizing information from these texts, or secondary sources. The child must understand that, if the information is very well stated in the text or if there is a lot of information to be gathered, it is okay to copy this information *verbatim* in one's notes if it is placed in quotation marks and if it will be paraphrased at a later point in the preparation of the composition. It is dismaying to hear from time to time of college students who do not understand these simple "rules of the game"—they honestly do not understand the educational and ethical ramifications involved in presenting verbatim, as one's own, material from another source.

How can you help your child learn how to say it in his or her own words? Let's suppose your child has the following bits of information selected from a chapter titled "The Future—Living in Space" and dealing with space colonies:

> The living area of the habitat will be a busy city, but one without skyscrapers or highways. Buildings will be on a human scale and positioned to create the longest sight lines. Architects will use every possible method to create the illusion of greater distances within the habitat.
>
> There will be a central plain around the whole tube and there will be many parks and open plazas. The whole colony will be bathed in cheerful sunlight, with lush trees and flowers growing everywhere.
>
> Buildings will be terraced up against the habitat's curved walls. The houses will be placed upon one another like layers of a wedding cake. Mechanical, electrical and plumbing facilities will all be hidden from view in the thick walls of the buildings and under the decks that form the ground.

You can first discuss with your child what the main point or idea of this passage is:

"Randy, what is this talking about?"

"What the colony will be like, you know, what it looks like."

"Do you think this author believes a space colony will be kind of a boring, dull-looking place?"

"No! It reminds me of how it would be on earth.."

"Me, too. In general, how could we describe what such a colony would look like?"

"Well, it says here that it will have buildings, like, and plumbing, and trees and flowers—*that's* really *strange!*"

"It is pretty far out. How could we describe this appearance in a sentence or two?"

"Let's see . . . Well, it looks a lot like earth, just like I said."

"Good—jot that down so we can work with it later. What else?"

"Well, it sounds like it would be pretty neat to live there."

"Yes, it does. Go ahead and write that down, too. It sounds like you were kind of surprised to find out how earth-like such a colony could be. Do you suppose most people would be surprised about this kind of description as well?"

"That's for sure. It sounds pretty far-fetched."

"That's true. Let's write that down, too. You know, I think you've got some good thoughts there to begin describing to the reader what a space colony might be like—what it might *have* to be like if people can really live there for any length of time."

Now, what has this parent accomplished with this brief discussion with Randy? Most important, of course, the central or main idea of this passage has been extracted and *paraphrased*. Saying it "in your own words" involves talking through the material— that is the only way children will learn how to paraphrase. What else has been accomplished? Whether this parent realized it or not, she helped Randy make a distinction between the *topic* of this passage and the *main idea*. The topic is what is being discussed in the passage, but the main idea may be—and usually is—more general, perhaps more abstract, but also *more important*. In other words, what is the more important idea about this passage: the description of the space colony or how the space colony will need to be very much like earth if it is to survive? Of course, the latter point is the main idea and this is what Randy will need to express in his report. How specific he gets in describing in his own words what the colony will look like will depend on a number of factors. Randy needs to understand, however, that if necessary, the bit about the hidden plumbing can be left out and the composition will not suffer; if he fails to mention the main idea, though, a fundamental concept about future space colonies may be lost to the reader.

Revising and Proofreading

After a couple of revising drafts of his report, Randy's opening paragraph on future space colonies—based on the above discussion—was as follows:

> You might be surprised to find out that space colonies may be a lot like earth. They might be very interesting and fun places to live and work in. In this report, I will explain *why* they would have to be like earth.

BACK TO BASICS

The rest of the report goes on with the stated explanation, and Randy uses some of the specific examples from the passage excerpted above as well as other passages to flesh out his explanations. The report is proofread and the final copy is prepared.

Let's take stock of what you can do with the report based on books and other reference materials. Before consulting a single piece of written material, you need to help your child narrow down or, if necessary, flesh out his or her topic. You brainstorm some questions, then refine them to a manageable core. Sources of information are then explored, selected, and abstracted based on the building questions. You then discuss the material in his or her own words.

You may be wondering how you will be able to come up with the kinds of questions that will generate and sustain your child's interest. This is a typical concern of parents. Interestingly, however, you will find that as you try these strategies more often with your child and become more aware *yourself* of how to think about new material to be read and written about, these questions will come more easily. In addition, they will get "better" in terms of how they focus or elaborate upon the information.

COMMUNICATION AS A FACILITATOR OF THE WRITING PROCESS

At this point it is necessary to highlight what may be a very obvious observation: Throughout these processes of helping your child to compose both "first-hand" and "book-based" reports, you have been continually *talking* to your child. This talking has been purposeful and interesting—for both of you. As our children grow older, so often the lines of communication become tangled, confused, and at their worst, broken down. Parents who are involved with their children in discussing and facilitating *learning* help to ensure that those lines stay intact and that their use is valuable *and trusted*.

You are also modeling a strategy for enquiry that will serve your child well throughout his or her life. As you explore together new ideas of knowledge, your child inevitably asks you questions. When your child was younger, you felt you had a fair degree of expertise in responding to these questions; now, however, you discover you know less and less! This is nothing to be ashamed of. In fact, when parents pretend as if they *do* know everything, the children find out very quickly indeed that "the emperor has no clothes"! It is far better to say, when confronted with a question about which you know little or nothing, "Gee, I don't know about that. Let's figure out how we can find out." Your subsequent strategy may be as simple as reminding the child that the question can be answered by consulting an encyclopedia. On the other hand, it may involve planning a trip to the library, checking with the reference librarian, dipping into the "Government Documents" section, and so on. *You* may not know where to begin. Model for your child what to do in such cases. Who do you get in touch with? Discuss possibilities with your child—you may decide for example that calling a particular office in the state government is a place to start. Regardless, do not leave your child with the response "I really don't know—why don't you go check that out?" You need to help them learn *how* to go about the process of "checking it out."

A delightful corollary to being involved this way in helping your child to learn is that *your* interest in learning is sustained. Through and with your child, you continue to learn. Parents are delighted to discover just how exhilarating this experience can be.

SPELLING AND HANDWRITING

As you think about how to respond to your child's mastery of spelling, you may find that it's necessary to revise some of your own notions about the way we spell words in English. Contrary to what many people believe, the best way to learn how to spell words is not through memorization. Good spellers are also good readers—but being a good reader does not guarantee good spelling. Words that we read must be used in writing. In addition, if we are simply curious about words—their many nuances of meaning and perhaps where they came from—we are usually good spellers.

Reading, writing, and curiosity—these are the ingredients of good spelling. People who combine these ingredients effectively have also learned a very important feature of English spelling: It makes sense. Although there are some rather strange and illogical spellings in our language, there are many more that are logical. The key is in knowing what to look for. Let's consider how you can help your upper elementary child understand how our spelling system makes sense.

Spelling does a very good job of representing *meaning*. Consider each of these words: *sign, muscle,* and *bomb.* Children often ask why there are "silent" letters in these words. It helps to pair up these words with other words in which these "silent" letters become "sounded": sign-signal, muscle-muscular, bomb-bombarded. These words are related in *meaning* and, therefore, the meaning "part" in each of them is spelled the same even though the pronunciation may change. Not all "silent" letters can be explained in this way, but many can.

Because so many words are related in meaning in the English language, it is a very nice feature indeed that their meaning is retained in their spelling. Some other examples may help to illustrate this point. Consider the following misspellings, and then see how thinking of a word related in meaning can help with the errors:

COMPATITION
COMBONATION
MENTLE

In each of these words, the spelling error occurs in a syllable where you hear an "uh" sound when you pronounce the word. This particular sound in words like these is quite troublesome, because quite simply sound is not a clue to the spelling. How can we help the children who made these errors remember the correct spellings? By requiring them to memorize each word? This works up to a point, but if we relied solely on memorization the system would break down after a while. *Meaning* is a much more powerful and long-lasting mnemonic.

Take the first error. This child should be shown a word related in spelling and in meaning to *competition: compete.* In *compete,* the sound in the second syllable is clearly heard—it is a "long e" sound—and the spelling of this sound is obvious. *Competition* comes from *compete,* of course, and although the pronunciation of the base word *compete* changes when the suffix *-ition* is added, the spelling does not change (except for dropping the final *e,* a principle that most students by this time have learned).

The same process is at work in the word *combination.* The child who misspelled this word should be shown the base word *combine,* from which *combination* is derived. Once again, the sound in the second syllable is clearly heard and the spelling apparent. When the suffix *-ation* is added, the spelling of the base does not change even though the pronunciation does.

How about MENTLE? A word related in meaning and in spelling which can explain the spelling is *mentality,* in which the sound is, once again, clearly heard and the spelling apparent.

Such errors as these—and the manner in which they can be corrected—demonstrate a fundamental and important principle of the spelling system of English: Words that are related in meaning are often related in spelling as well, despite changes in sound. Once children begin to understand this principle, they develop the habit of trying to think of a related word when they are stumped about a particular spelling. Their reasoning will be something like this:

"Hmmm. I'm not sure of the spelling of the second syllable in 'courage.' Let's see. Is there another word similar to 'courage'? Ah, yes, there *is* one. It's *courageous.* I can hear a long *a* sound in the second syllable, so I'll try the letter *a* and see how it looks. . . ."

Although this reading may not be articulated in quite this way by the child, our imaginary train of thought does represent a process that can occur at some level. And remember, it is a process that will stay with your child from here on out and which can serve, as the following example illustrates, as a foundation for vocabulary development through knowledge about word structure.

BACK TO BASICS

From time to time, when your child shares his or her school compositions with you, note any spelling errors that might serve as a basis for taking advantage of the role of *meaning* in spelling.

For example, a fifth-grade boy named Jeff spelled "condemn" as CONDEM. Jeff's problem was with the "silent" *n*. A word that explains this spelling—and in which the "n" *does* stand for a sound—is condemnation. Although Jeff had not heard of the word *condemnation*, his parents used it to do two things:

1. They pointed out why the spelling of *condemn* has the "silent" *n*—because spelling preserves meaning;
2. Jeff's vocabulary was extended—he was able to understand the meaning of the new word "condemnation" because he already knew the word *condemn*.

This second point is perhaps the more important. Because spelling preserves the meaning among words that are related, it can become a significant source of vocabulary knowledge for students. You can help your upper-elementary child become aware of how spelling and vocabulary are really two faces of the same coin. In so doing, you will help him in developing an attitude that considers words with interest, with curiosity, and with a valuable payoff in learning.

What about *handwriting* at the upper elementary level? As with the younger children, neat and legible handwriting is desirable *in the appropriate context*. Some instruction will be given over in school to reviewing letter formation in cursive writing. The application of this knowledge should be in the final written products that a child creates. These "final products," by the way, are not necessarily formal reports or stories; they may be notes and the phone messages mentioned earlier. Whenever the audience is other than oneself, however, the handwriting should be legible. Once again, it is important to mention that it should not be expected that the handwriting should look like the models in a handwriting booklet. If the composition is in fact going to be bound in a book to be placed in the library, then the child may strive for a script that comes very close to the model. Otherwise, the criterion is legibility with a minimum of strain on the writer.

Many children at the upper elementary level can become quite proficient typists; most of these children are amazingly adept at moving along at a pretty good clip using only two fingers—the "hunt and peck" method polished to a high gloss! If your child is interested in typing, however, his or her motivation may sustain learning the standard "touch typing" method. If you have a microcomputer, you may purchase some very fine programs for teaching touch typing; these programs afford appropriately paced lessons, monitor performance on an ongoing basis, and keep tabs on an individual's "word-per-minute" rate. Because most students will eventually be expected to type most of their compositions—as well as perform a number of tasks on computers thus requiring keyboard familiarity—learning this skill in the upper elementary grades is quite beneficial. It bears repeating, however, that this should be undertaken only if the child is sufficiently motivated. He or she may be quite happy to "hunt and peck"; far better to tolerate this strategy and have the child remain interested in writing and the keyboard than to press for systematic typing instruction and drive the child away entirely.

SUMMARY

In this chapter we have discussed the role of the writing process—prewriting, writing, revising, and proofreading—in different types of writing:

1. *"Personal" Reports.* These compositions develop your child's ability to organize and present information on a topic that he or she understands.
2. *Reports Based on New Information.* These compositions develop your child's ability to obtain new information from a first-hand source, to organize, and to present this information.
3. *Reports Based on Books and Other Reference Materials.* Once your child is comfortable with the first two types of reports, he or she is better able to select materials and obtain information from those materials. This information is then organized and written up in the report.

BACK TO BASICS

Importantly, the "basics" of spelling and handwriting will be better appreciated and mastered by your child because the emphasis is on the *functional* role of these skills. When your child's writing is received and appreciated by a definite audience, then these skills assume their rightful importance.

Your role in your child's development of writing at the upper elementary level is:

1. *Communicate* with your child through discussion and questions.
2. *Model* an inquisitive strategy for obtaining information and thinking about that information.
3. *Respond* to your child's writing by serving as a "sounding board" for ideas expressed in the writing and as a "proofreader" for the draft prior to the final draft.

You may not be a literary critic, but if you support and facilitate your upper elementary child's writing in the ways described in this chapter, you will help your child to be well on his or her way to purposeful and effective writing.

CHAPTER **10** Arithmetic

Arithmetic is intriguing and exciting as another human communication source. Fear of arithmetic hinders this genuine expression.

As YOUR CHILD moves into fourth grade his or her life in the arithmetic arena becomes more complicated because of the complexity of the arithmetic content. Much of the content is built upon previous learning, but the complexity is greater. If your child seems to be having difficulty with any activity it is essential to ask yourself what are the antecedent learnings necessary to accomplish the present task? You must then return to these tasks and redevelop them with your child through activities.

ROUNDING AND ESTIMATING NUMBERS

One school activity that often gives children trouble is that of rounding and estimating. This activity is based on knowledge of place value and a sense of whether a number is closer to its beginning sequence or ending sequence (place value). For example, in the numeral 43, the three is closer to the beginning (40) than to the end (50). Therefore, it would be rounded to 40.

While working with your child, try to relate the concept of estimating and rounding to everyday life. This can be done with money. For example, when grocery shopping, you can involve your child by saying: "I've collected these three items: bread, $1.43, margarine, $.98, and jelly, $1.20. I have $4.00, will I have enough money? How much do you think I'll need?" Stop right there and say, "See, the margarine is closest to $1.00, so we can round the $.98 to $1.00. The jelly is closer to $1.00 than it is to $2.00, so there's another dollar. Now, what about the bread? Is it closer to $1.00 or $2.00?" Let your child tell you it is closer to $1.00 than it is to $2.00. Why? Because if it were $1.50, you would round up and call it $2.00. So by rounding off you and your child should estimate that you will need about $3.00. In actuality, you'll need close to $4.00.

To do this activity one time is certainly not sufficient to accomplish a firm feeling for rounding and estimating. Look for things in everyday life that reinforce the concept. For example, the merchandising technique of making items approximately two cents or two dollars less than a complete sequence is a prime example of the need for rounding to get a true sense of the price of items. You know, the pickup truck that is base priced at $5,995, not $6,000; the maple syrup that is $1.99 a pint instead of $2.00.

When you see these obvious examples, call them to your child's attention. When you gather items into your grocery basket, hand your child the pocket or purse calculator and suggest that he or she round off each item and enter it into the calculator. Tell him or her to round to the nearest dollar. (Have you noticed that you can just about figure a dollar per item and be close to what you'll spend at the checkstand?) So, as you place an item into the basket, say, "Soup, $.75." Have him or her say: "$1.00." As you approach the checkout counter ask him or her to give you a total. Check the rounded estimates against the actual bill. In the preceding example, be aware that the level of estimating is fairly gross. That is, the $.75 could have been rounded to $.80 for a finer level of accuracy. The level of accuracy you will accept should be determined by the child's level of abilities at this point in time.

Estimating the final answer to a problem is an essential element in solving word problems. To arrive at a defensible estimate of the answer, the child must have a sense of the computational procedures to follow. Another advantage to estimating is to check the relative accuracy of the actual computation. If the two answers are too disparate, the child should be alerted to the need to examine the computational process chosen, "Did I multiply when I should have divided?" or the accuracy of the computation.

You, the parent, should estimate answers to problems for your child by verbalizing the steps you go through as you arrive at a solution. For example: "It's one hundred miles to home. At fifty-five miles per hour it should take a little less than two hours because there are two fifties in one hundred."

MAKING CHANGE

Another problem area in arithmetic is that of making change. Relatively little time is devoted to this activity in school but it is one each of us, even as adults, should handle well. Today's modern cash registers tell the clerk how much change to give. But it is well to anticipate your change so you are in agreement with the amount you receive.

It is essential to have your child add back toward the sum given to the clerk. For example, if the item is $1.64 and a $5.00 bill is handed over, the change is easily figured by adding back to the whole number $5.00 (or 500 in computing the example). The mental process would go something like this: "A dollar sixty-four plus six cents makes a dollar seventy. A dollar seventy plus thirty cents (twenty-five and five cents) makes two dollars. Two dollars plus three dollars makes the five dollars. I should get back three dollars, a quarter and possibly two nickels and a penny."

This activity should be practiced by your child and you. The mental process should be practiced verbally for you to listen to the strategy your child uses. Use this activity when your child wants to purchase an object. Suggest to your child that he or she go through the process before the object is actually purchased. Start with relatively simple computations like $.83 from $1.00.

The process of making change will also help your child if he or she is having difficulty in handling mental subtraction. For example, if the teacher requests the answer to something like 400 take away 384, it is much easier to add up to 400 than to do the process of regrouping from the tens column. Rather, the child can say, "384 plus one is 385. 385 plus 15 is 400. The answer is 16."

WORD PROBLEMS

Earlier, in the first chapter on mathematics the authors talked about word problems. These problems will be encountered by your child through all the grades; in fact, all through life. We cannot emphasize strongly enough the need to practice these problems.

If you are to help your child with these problems it would be well to find some of them in your child's arithmetic text and dissect them for the essential word elements that reveal the operations that are to be performed. Note that terms like "in all," "how many," "the total" indicate the need to add, while "less than," "more than," "greater than," "much farther" usually indicate the need to subtract.

Continue to pursue word problems with your child by using them in daily life. Even if the mathematical complexity is not great, what you are striving for is the wording. To this end, ask your child: "I have four eggs, this cake calls for nine. How many more do I need?" "So you want pizza for dinner? Well, I have $3.00, your Dad has $3.00, and you have $2.00. A pizza is $9.00. Do we have enough? If not, how much more do we need?" This is a two-step problem requiring both addition and subtraction.

Be sure to have your child make up his or her own word problems. This strategy is of a higher order than merely solving such a problem because it requires the child to decide on the computational process or processes to be used, generate the situation, and solve the problem. Nonetheless, these are valuable skills in developing the ability to cope with true-life word problems.

THE GEOMETRIC JUNGLE

Beginning at approximately third grade your child may begin to encounter the terminology of geometry if the teacher has made an effort to touch on all elements of the mathematics curriculum or all of the chapters in the textbook. Too often, however, teachers are so busy coping with the needs of the wide range of intellectual abilities, that geometric terms may not be addressed until later grades. Once introduced, the child will find the terminology new and strange. You can narrow the gap between terminology and experience by introducing the terms and concepts in your daily life.

To introduce the term "line segment," which is the shortest straight line between two points, you might have your child experience the axiom "the shortest distance between two points is a straight line." For example, suggest that your child count the steps between several objects at the park by walking from the sandbox to the slide, to the drinking fountain. Have him or her count the steps as the route is followed. Then, suggest he or she count the steps by walking directly from the sandbox to the drinking fountain. When he or she tells you the distance you can verbalize, "so a line segment is the shortest path between two points." This may seem a little artificial and contrived but it is an attempt to get the words into your child's vocabulary via a concrete experience.

Similarly, the terms "radius" and "diameter" can be introduced experientially. These terms refer to a circle and the appropriate line segments. Again, experientially, a pizza would be a good learning encounter for the terms diameter and radius. Ask your child to put a toothpick into the very center of the pizza. Tell him you are going to cut the pizza across the diameter. Show that the diameter goes directly through the center and touches both sides of the circle. Make your cut but leave the two halves together. Next, state you will now cut the pizza along the radius. Make a big point of placing the point of the knife at the very center while the toothpick is still marking the spot. Now, cut from the center to the edge. State that the line from the center to the edge is a radius. Ask your child how big a piece he or she wants and have him or her help you place the knife along the radius to be cut. Reinforce the idea that no matter how big a piece is cut, the line from the center to the edge is always the radius. Without completely spoiling the joy of pizza eating, don't forget the fraction lessons that can be reviewed with halves, quarters, eighths, etc. ENJOY!

CALCULATOR—OR NO CALCULATOR

Should you permit your child to use a calculator? Yes, is the qualified answer. Why qualified? Because the use of a calculator has many practical applications, especially after the basic mathematical functions have been learned well. Even in the earlier years when the concept of place value is being learned the calculator can help your child develop a sense of the order of the place value of the numerals by doing such simple exercises as adding 1+1+1 until the 9 is reached. The next addition triggers the two-digit numeral we call 10, with the numerals in their proper positions.

Again, in the earlier grades the use of the operational symbols are reinforced by using the calculator because the child must use the symbols to accomplish the operation. For example, to accomplish the division operation of twelve divided by four, the child must think the steps: twelve divided by, pushing the division sign, then the numeral 4, then he or she must think equals, and push the equal sign.

Another advantage to the calculator is the ability to shorten the cumbersome computations necessary to arrive at a solution to a sequential problem. For example, to solve the question of how many times the heart beats in a month, the child can concentrate on the steps rather than on the actual mechanics of multiplying. The solution sequence verbalized might go something like this: "Let's see, they say the heart beats about seventy-two times a minute, and there are sixty minutes in an hour and twenty-four hours in a day, and about thirty-one days in a month, so I'd multiply $72 \times 60 \times 24 \times 31$; ah ha, 3,214,080 beats in a month."

The wise parent will use the child's fascination with the ease and speed of the calculator to regularly involve the child in daily life questions such as the supermarket advertisement that offers you six cans of a product at one price compared with the regular price. The question to be addressed is how much of a savings may be accomplished by buying the item on sale even if it is necessary to buy six items instead of only one.

It can be a real lesson in modern-day economics to ask the question: "If I buy the jumbo size of detergent can I save more than buying an equal quantity (by weight) of two smaller sizes?"

It is amazing (more to us than to the child) to discover that quite often the two smaller sizes are less expensive.

In summary, the authors believe learning to use the calculator is a highly profitable activity for the child especially after the basic number operations are well learned.

EFFECTIVE SCHOOLS AND CLASSROOMS

In a cognitive, skill-laden subject such as arithmetic, research has shown the need for, and the efficacy of, certain procedures. In this last section on helping your child in arithmetic the authors want to briefly discuss these procedures and suggest that if you find yourself directly involved in supplementing the classroom instruction, you too should implement these procedures.

HOMEWORK REVIEW

The first of these procedures is to review the homework that was given and returned to your child. If none was given or returned, it may be necessary for you to parallel the classroom instruction and to provide homework for your child. You can choose a number of problems from the child's textbook or make up some which illustrate the skill to be learned. It is wise to institute a structured study time and an appropriate study place for this homework review.

The first thing you do is correct the homework and review the skill to be learned. This would sound something like this: "Yesterday we were learning to find the missing numeral in a sentence similar to this: $n + 12 = 21$. To do this we . . ."

From here the next step in the sequence is the introduction of new content. This is done by relating the new material to prerequisite skills and concepts. This might begin with: "You remember when we learned that addition is the opposite of subtraction and that you can 'undo' addition by subtracting? And so in the sentence $n + 12 = 21$ we can find 'n' by . . ."

Following this review you introduce the new content with concrete materials and examples. By this we mean to use real items,

149

manipulative counters, or real life examples. From this introduction of content you proceed to controlled practice. The controlled practice is where your child works a number of examples under your guidance and monitoring. This is best done by having him or her verbalize the steps as they are done. Be sure to remain silent as the child verbalizes the steps unless it is absolutely essential to interrupt. If your monitoring demonstrates that it is necessary, repeat examples and expand on the meaning steps. If your child has the idea, you should provide examples for practice. These should be only enough to reinforce the learning. Remember, the same content is being taught at school.

Finally, regular reviews of previous learning is essential if the skills are to be maintained at a utilitarian level.

CLASSROOM QUALITIES

It should be mentioned that those schools and classrooms producing high scores on achievement tests are characterized by a number of qualities. They have:

- A clear focus on academic goals
- Little waste time in getting lessons started
- Children who are kept working toward a goal in well-ordered classrooms
- Few interruptions of lessons
- Teachers who use diagnostic, re-teach strategies
- Teachers whose lessons are well planned, proceeding from an organized start to conclusion
- Quick academic feedback on success or failure
- More whole group instruction than small group unless providing remediation
- Content broken into small learning steps
- Less time devoted to classroom management

The foregoing are a few hallmarks of classroom practices that produce high achievment. We include these so that you may be aware of the hallmarks of classroom practices that bring about high mathematic achievement.

150

MATHEMATICS ANXIETY

Math anxiety is found in humans from nine years old to sixty-five years old, and probably earlier and later. Math anxiety is a real sense of tension as a person approaches a math-related problem. How many of us would rather not balance our checkbooks? How long do we delay the task just because we *know* the balance is not going to agree with what the bank says we have? Math anxiety is a debilitating inner fear of failure. It has its roots in the very nature of mathematics and the teaching that is supposed to promote the skill. Math does not tolerate close answers. Math as a subject insists on right answers. After all, $7 + 5 = 12$, not 11, not 13. The child who gets an arithmetic paper turned back with five or ten problems marked wrong is immediately informed he or she can't do math. This implies to the child that something is wrong with him or her. Another factor said to contribute to math anxiety is that speed in computation is essential. You must be able to perform the operations in order to arrive at the final answer before it is time to collect the papers.

Another contributing factor is what researchers call the "sudden death" syndrome. It is this awareness in the child that he or she just can't possibly understand a particular concept. Everyone else can get it (he or she thinks) but he or she just can't do it. The child is too shy or too intimidated to ask a question or to appear foolish. "Oh, if someone would only ask why . . ." the child thinks as the teacher says, "Are there any questions? No? O.K., get to work."

It has been said that the fluently verbal child may find mathematics ambiguous rather than exact because of the strange results in such areas as fractions. If you multiply fractions you end up with smaller ones. If you divide you get larger ones.

Finally, math disability is cumulative. One must be able to perform the operations of addition to multiply, to multiply and subtract in order to divide. Once the cycle of disability begins, it is difficult to break.

Math anxiety produces a sense of poor self-esteem which results in poor performance and further underachievement. This in turn reinforces the anxiety level in doing math.

BACK TO BASICS

The topic of math anxiety is an important one, especially in view of today's need for mathematically literate workers. The prevalence of this anxiety is such that whole classes in colleges and universities have been devoted to helping students cope with math anxiety. A pertinent book on the subject, should you wish to read more, is *Overcoming Math Anxiety*, by Sheila Tobias.

SUMMARY

It is for all of the above reasons that we have urged you as parents to make your interactions with your child as enjoyable, as low key, and as non-threatening as possible. It is not essential in these interactions that the right answer be obtained before you put aside the activity.

As you seek to help your child progress in school, you need to be sensitive to the personalities of the teachers he or she has or will have. When you attend the school open house make an effort to talk to the teachers in the next grade your child will enter. Ask questions in conversational tones like, "What math topics are covered in this grade? What is your favorite subject? How do you feel about departmentalizing in the elementary grades?" What you are seeking are clues to the teachers' attitude toward mathematics. There have been a number of studies to show that parental and teacher attitude definitely affect the child's attitude toward a subject. Be sure to talk with other parents about the classroom personality of the teachers your child will encounter. When you find there is a teacher who has a reputation for being brusque, possibly impatient with children who have difficulty, request the principal to place your child in a different classroom. If you do it early in the year preceding next year's assignment of children to teachers you will usually have no trouble.

Once again, it is you, the loving, caring parent, who can help make the success of your child possible through your constant interactions and awareness of what is happening in the day to day school life of your child as he or she moves through the grades.

PART FIVE
Prologue

CHAPTER 11 Parent-School-Student Partnership

The parent-school-student partnership is a unique and vital feature of American education. This partnership working together will solve the problems that affect the education of all children.

IN MANY SCHOOL districts today decision making is far removed from parents. Their only decision may be in the form of voting for school board members or boards of trustees and mill levies or bond issues. It is more worthwhile to have parents help in decision making at the curriculum and codes of conduct level as well.

Historically, when one viewed education of an earlier time period in the United States, the right to determine the child's curriculum was considered an undeniable right of each parent. As the school systems became more and more complex, it developed from an itinerant teacher traveling from home to home into a one-room school and finally to the multifaceted educational systems of today. Many parents have been left out of the organizational structure and curriculum planning. Because of the need for more communication with parents, professional educators have been recommending procedures for reaching out to parents in an effort to get them more involved in today's schools.

BACK TO BASICS

Many educators have recommended that a parent organization be formed in each school. This organized parent-school-student partnership would allow its members to reexamine the status of their own schools and to take steps toward revitalizing and extending the effectiveness of the parent-school-student partnership. This organization of concerned people would play a large part in the solution of problems that ultimately affect the welfare of their children.

Even if an organization does not exist and the likelihood of getting one going is not possible, you still need to become involved in the education of your child because closer ties are needed between the home and the school.

CLOSER TIES BETWEEN HOME AND SCHOOL

Professional educators and parents have recognized for years the need for closer ties between the home and the school. As these ties are developed, the children will benefit greatly through this added cooperation and interest.

As mentioned many times in this book, the first teacher is the parent in the home. These first teaching experiences will go into the school with your child as well as all other assistance that you give your child while in school. Also, the school will be expanding its teaching experiences into your home. This reciprocity of effort is essential so that everyone will know what to expect and how to help your child benefit most from this cooperative effort.

COMMUNICATION AND INVOLVEMENT

Communication and involvement are the focal points of an effective partnership. Communication is a very important human need, and this is especially true in a parent-school-child partnership. It is imperative that each one in the partnership knows what is expected. Through communication, role clarification can be determined, which is a very important step for working together in harmony.

Communication does not mean coming to school only when your child experiences some difficulty! Communication *does* mean coming to school throughout the year at various times to discuss successes as well as problems your child has. If you cannot come to school, communication can be through the telephone, through written messages, or through a home visit by the teacher.

Involvement means displaying a willingness to assist your child's teacher in the dozens of small ways a busy parent can show interest. For example, do you have time to donate one hour a day to come to school and help grade papers? Do you have handicraft skills you can teach small groups of children while the teacher works with other children? Do you have subject matter knowledge you can share with the children at their grade level? Can you construct learning carrels where children can sit and work independently of their peers? Are you willing to provide the cookies for the next class party? Perhaps you haven't the time to bake them, but can you buy them? Can you sew costumes for the class play? make puppets? Could you offer to make the next bulletin board or just cut out the letters from a pattern to help the teacher? Are you willing to give up a weekend to help with a field trip the class is taking?

Your interest in helping the busy teacher as he or she teaches your child communicates to that child that the business of education is serious, valued, and supported by a parent who has many, many demands, but who always has a bit of time for school.

If you *are* able to arrange your own schedule so that you have time that you can volunteer, so much the better. Being a volunteer in the school will keep you well informed about the school operations and what is being required of your child. Through research in the area of parent volunteers, it has been determined that the work of the volunteer will affect the teacher and school as much as this work will influence you and your child.

Usually, the major involvement parents have in the school is when they participate as an audience for a school function or a back-to-school or open house program. This audience role is an important one. This not only supports the child as a participant in the varied programs offered in school, but it also informs parents of school activities, needs, and coming events.

Another aspect of parental involvement is assisting the child with homework assignments. Through your supervision of the work that comes home, you are learning what goes on at school and helping your child meet the school objectives. Work done by the teacher in the school can be easily undone by the parent if the values promoted at school are not reinforced at home.

SELF-CONCEPT

As the partnership among parent-school-student is developed, the child's self-concept is strengthened. How your child thinks and feels about him or herself depends upon the successes that your child accomplishes not only in education but also in many other aspects of his or her life. However, through research efforts, a very clear relationship has been established between the child's self-concept and the effectiveness with which he or she learns. Children with positive self-concepts perform better and achieve at higher levels than do children who have poor self-concepts. It is obvious that parents need to help in the development of good self-concepts in their child.

Since the child's self-concept is developed from the way others have acted toward him or her, you need to recognize your child's unique qualities and act upon them in a positive way. The building of this wholesome concept of the self becomes increasingly important as your child has more contact outside the home. You as the key adult in your child's life will have an everlasting effect through your love, understanding, and acceptance of your child as he or she comes into contact with other children and adults. This is especially true as your child becomes involved with school activities and feels the need for educational achievement. If your child perceives himself or herself as a capable learner, your child will develop a positive self-concept. As this book has constantly pointed out, it is through your assistance as you help your child succeed in educational pursuits that his or her self-concept will indeed reach higher levels.

It is essential for your child's self-concept that your child experience success. Therefore, in helping your child with school activities, it is very important to start at a low or easy level of difficulty whether it be in the area of reading, writing, or arithmetic. The mastery of these lower level skills will indeed enhance and sustain a positive self-concept. It is not a waste of time to practice on these low level skills. If interest is high in the subject, higher levels of materials can be undertaken. Be sure to establish realistic goals for your child so success can be achieved most of the time.

Allow your child to make decisions that will affect his educational studies and to make choices in his or her life. Not only will your child enjoy this type of decision-making but this will also aid in developing a positive self-concept that will make him or her feel worthy and capable. Children who are often put down or not allowed to make decisions usually develop poor self-concepts and become less involved and enthusiastic.

Role modeling is an essential part for developing a good self-concept in your child. For example, when you approach a task with confidence, your "I can do it" or "we can do it" attitude is communicated to the child and in turn strengthens your child's attitude "I *can*." A parent who has a good self-concept will be a great help in developing a healthy self-concept in his or her child as well.

Another vital way to improve the self-concept of your child is through assisting him or her in the communication skills. Your child's ability to speak, write, listen, and use the communication skills of mathematics and reading can be a vital factor in developing a good self-concept. This book has given you many ideas to assist you in these areas. It is through this social interaction with you and other human beings that your child develops a positive self-concept.

SUMMARY

Parental involvement in the school enlarges and facilitates the communication process among parents, teachers, and the school

administrator. Parental attitudes and behaviors toward the
school, and toward children as learners, are enhanced through
parent involvement in the school. These attitudes and behaviors
are not uni-directional. As teachers and administrators sense the
interest, support, and concerns of parents, so too do they gain a
renewed sense of dedication and concern for a safe, happy, and
constructive learning environment for each child.

The active cooperative efforts by parents, teachers, and others
influence the educational environment and experiences of children in positive and productive ways which result in better self-
concepts and increased academic achievement.

As you have noticed, we have concluded with a prologue rather
than with an epilogue because this is the commencement of your
child's lifelong learning.

*You can and will make a difference in your child's success in
school.*